Student Supplement to Accompany Educational Psychology: Classroom Connections

Second Edition

Sample Test Items with Answers
Feedback on All Margin Note Questions
Guidelines for Using Case Studies
Observation Guides

Paul Eggen
University of North Florida

Don Kauchak
University of Utah

Merrill, an imprint of
Macmillan College Publishing Company
New York

Maxwell Macmillan Canada
Toronto

Maxwell Macmillan International
New York Oxford Singapore Sydney

Cover art: Paul Klee, courtesy of Galerie Beyeler, Basel

Printed in the United States of America

Macmillan College Publishing Company
866 Third Avenue
New York, New York 10022

Macmillan College Publishing Company is part of the
Maxwell Communication Group of Companies.

Maxwell Macmillan Canada, Inc.
1200 Eglinton Avenue East, Suite 200
Don Mills, Ontario M3C 3N1

ISBN: 0-02-331691-8

Printing: 1 2 3 4 5 6 7 8 9   Year: 4 5 6 7 8

INCREASING YOUR LEARNING:
A VALUE-ADDED PACKAGE OF TEXT SUPPLEMENTS

Dear Students,

Having been students ourselves for many years, we understand your experiences as you take courses and study different texts. All authors' goals in writing books are for you to learn as much as possible from your study, and this is our goal as well. In order to help you reach that goal, we are including this package with your new text in an effort to help you in your growth as a developing professional. We sincerely hope that you will find the package helpful and that it will make your study both in the course and in field experiences more meaningful.

The package exists in four parts which are outlined as follows:

Part I: Analyzing Case Studies: Suggestions and Guidelines

Since each of the chapters in the text begins with a *case study,* the first section offers some guidelines for analyzing case studies. Hopefully, these guidelines will make your analysis of case studies more meaningful and will increase your understanding of the text content.

Part II: Answers to Margin Questions

To help put you in an active role as you study the text, we have included a number of questions in the margins of each of the chapters. The questions ask you to relate the text content to your life as you're now living it, to relate different topics of the text to each other, and to help you apply text content to classroom situations. Part II gives you our answers to these questions.

Part III: Practice Test Questions

Research indicates that achievement is increased when students have a chance to practice with the kind of items they might face on tests and quizzes. Part III offers you a series of practice test questions for each of the chapters in the text. The practice questions are similar in format and difficulty to those you might see on actual tests. Answers and brief discussions of each of the items are included.

Part IV: Observing in Classrooms: Exercises and Activities

Some of you will be involved in field experiences or clinical activities that are associated with the course you're taking, and you may not have been in a public or private school classroom since you were a student. To help you get as much as possible from your field experiences, Part IV offers a set of suggestions for observing teachers and interviewing both teachers and students.

Again, we hope that you will find these supplements useful and that they will increase your understanding of the material in the text.

Good luck in your study.

Paul Eggen

Paul Eggen

Don Kauchak

Don Kauchak

Table of Contents

Part I
Analyzing Case Studies: Suggestions and Guidelines

As you read this text, you will see that each chapter begins with a case study (commonly called a "case"), and chapters 2 through 13 also end with case studies. Cases are written accounts of actual classroom episodes. They include a description of the teacher's and students' behaviors, and dialogue that took place during the episode is presented as it occurred. In a sense, case studies read like short stories about classroom incidents. The fact that each incident is on paper allows us to study the teacher's and students' behaviors in detail. We can examine different parts as many times as we want, and we can study and discuss these parts in depth.

Though case studies are somewhat like short stories, they differ in two important respects. First, short stories are fictional, whereas case studies are based on real classroom experiences. Second, specific case studies have been selected because the teachers' and students' behaviors in them illustrate (or violate) the principles of learning and teaching that are presented in the text.

Because cases contain information that illustrates important ideas, they must be read with more care and concentration that would be needed to read a short story or novel. To facilitate this process, some simple techniques can be used to help you learn more from each case than you would learn if you only read them casually.

The purpose in preparing this part of the package and including it with the text is to offer you some suggestions that will make your examination of case studies more meaningful. As your ability to analyze cases improves, your understanding of the content in the text will increase, and hopefully, your ability to assess your own teaching will also increase.

Focusing on the beginning-of-chapter cases, the techniques can be outlined in the following four steps:

1) *Skim the case study.*

   The purpose in the first step is to give you an overall feel for the episode. If, for example, the case illustrates a teacher trying to help his or her students learn some content, you will identify the topic and what—in general—the teacher did to help the students understand the topic. At this point in your reading, you are not expected to recognize some of the subtle or sophisticated actions of the teacher. Skimming the case study should take only a matter of minutes.

2) *Read the case a second time, and make a written list of behaviors the teacher or students displayed that you believe are significant.*

   The second step is important to learning the most from cases. Remember, cases are presented for a purpose, and much—but not all—of the information in them illustrates noteworthy teacher or student behaviors. The process of making a decision about what is significant and what isn't is the critical part of your study. You won't know until you've read the chapter whether or not the items you've included are the most significant ones, but the decision making process will make your study much more meaningful. As you gain experience in analyzing cases, you'll improve in your ability to predict the significance of a behavior. The items on the list can be tersely stated and written in outline form. Preparing the list should not be time consuming or laborsome.

3) *Read the chapter, relating your list to the topics as you read. Add items to the list that you didn't originally include.*

   As you read, keep the list you've prepared at your side for easy reference, relating the items on the list to the section you're reading. Check off items on your list as you read, making notes and adding additional items that you realize are significant.

4) *Examine unchecked items on the list.*

   Look again at your list and ask yourself why items you originally believed to be important turned out to be insignificant. They may simply be unimportant, or they may be significant but not in the context of the present chapter. Your analysis of these items will further increase your understanding of the chapter.

To illustrate these four steps, let's look at the case study that introduces chapter 7, "Cognitive Views of Learning." Then let's apply the steps to the case.

David Shelton is preparing a unit on the solar system for his ninth-grade earth science class. He took from his filing cabinet a color transparency showing the sun throwing "globs" of gases off into space. He then assembled a large model of the solar system illustrating the planets in their orbital planes, their sizes, their relative distances from the sun, and suspended it from the ceiling of his classroom. Finally he duplicated a matrix for the students, which had the planets' names across the top, and the orbital plane, size, distance from the sun, period of rotation, and length of year down the left side. (See page 302 of the text for the actual matrix.)

David spent the first day of his unit having the students examine the transparency with the "globs." He also demonstrated throwing off the "globs" by tying one pair of athletic socks to a 3-foot piece of string and another pair to a 5-foot piece of string, whirling the two around his head simultaneously to demonstrate that they revolved around his head on the same plane. He asked the students to relate his demonstration to the transparency and then had the students compare the planets in his model to each other. They added information to their charts as they compared different items of information.

After students identified the asteroid belt in his model, he had Mary Anne be the "sun" and Kevin be the "Earth." He directed Kevin to revolve around the "sun" as the Earth would, and he then moved in an exaggerated elliptical path around Mary Anne to illustrate the orbit of comets. The class then compared the planets, asteroids, and comets, and David finished the lesson with a brief discussion of meteors.

He began the second day of the unit by saying, "To review, I want you to work with your partner and write down as much as you can about what we learned yesterday. You have 3 minutes. Go ahead."

The room quickly became a buzz of voices and scratching on papers as different pairs conferred and wrote down what they remembered.

He then asked several of the pairs to report their results. In the process Laura and Jim stated, "Venus is called the Earth's twin."

"Good," David smiled, "Gee, I wonder why that might be the case. Why do you think so? . . . Randy?"

". . ."

"Randy?"

Randy almost jumped, suddenly realizing that he had drifted off and hadn't heard David's question.

"Did you hear the question or would you like me to repeat it?"

"I'm sorry, Mr. Shelton. Would you repeat it please?"

"Why do you suppose Venus is called the Earth's twin?"

". . ."

"Go ahead and look at your chart."

". . . It's about the same size as the Earth," Randy responded hesitantly after studying his chart.

"Yes. Good."

Randy decided he'd better start taking notes to keep himself from drifting away again.

"Remember, everyone," David continued, "the information we're learning should make sense to us. Just like Randy's comment. Venus isn't called the Earth's twin for no reason. It's because they're about the same size. Be sure you always ask yourself WHY each of the things we learn is true.

". . . Okay. What else?"

"Pluto wasn't part of the original solar system," Juan volunteered.

"Interesting comment, Juan. Go on."

"I was watching 'Nova' with my Mom, and they said that they think that Pluto was floating around and the solar system sort of grabbed it."

"Now, that's really interesting. Let's everybody think about that and look at our model and the transparency (showing the 'globs' thrown off the sun), and see what might relate to that idea."

David paused for several seconds and then said, "What do you think, Angela?"

". . ."

"Where is Pluto located?"

". . . Out there," Angela responded pointing to Pluto on the model.

"Yes. It's the planet farthest from the sun. . . . Does that support or detract from what Juan said?"

". . . Supports," Lori volunteered.

"How?" David nodded, gesturing for her to continue.

". . . If it were captured from somewhere else, it makes sense that it would be the last one."

"What if it was captured before some of the others were made?" Alfredo asked.

"That's an interesting question, Alfredo. Let's think about that one everyone. What else do we know about Pluto? . . . Look at the model. . . . Sylvia."

". . . It isn't in line with the others," Sylvia said, motioning with her hand to indicate that its orbital plane was different from the others.

"Its path is funny, too," Juan added. "Sometimes it's actually inside Neptune's."

"And what did we call the 'paths'?" David probed.

"Orbits," several of the students responded in unison.

"Okay. Excellent, everyone. See how this relates to what I said a minute ago. Now we see how Pluto's location and orbit relates to its possible origin," David continued "thinking aloud" for the students.

"Now, what else do we know about Pluto that might relate to our discussion? . . . Jeff?"

". . ."

"What about Pluto's size?"

". . . It's the smallest, I think."

"Yes, very good, and Mercury is the second smallest. And how might that be related?"

". . . It would be easier to capture than if it was big," Jeff responded.

David continued the discussion for a few more minutes, had the students summarize what they had discussed, and then he said, "Okay, everyone. You've done an excellent job of gathering and relating items of information about the solar system. Now, I have a short assignment. I want you to write a paragraph describing how the Earth became a member of the solar system and comparing that to how Pluto became a member. Use the information we've discussed for the last two days.

"Now remember," David emphasized, "the information must be in a paragraph. You cannot merely write down isolated sentences."

"Everybody ready? . . . Good. You should easily finish by the end of the period. I'll come around and answer questions. Go ahead and start now."

Randy sat there for a moment, trying to get started. Mercury—the smallest. No, is that what Mr. Shelton said? He turned to Karen and said, "Did Mr. Shelton say Mercury was the smallest planet?"

"No, Pluto. It's the smallest and farthest away. Mercury's the second smallest," Karen responded.

"Okay. Pluto," Randy thought to himself. "Solar system. . . . Sun . . . Pluto. . . . Smallest. Far away. . . . The Earth. Third one. . . . Orbital plane. What's that got to do with it? Oh, yeah. Something about globs from the sun. I think I get it."

He then began writing.

Juan was also attempting to organize his thoughts for the assignment. "Okay," he thought to himself. "The Earth came off the sun with all the other globs. . . . So, its orbit is on the same plane as the others. . . . They made the solar system. The sun's gravity keeps them in orbit. Pluto's isn't, . . . so it came from somewhere else. Also, it's little, so it's easy to capture by the sun's gravity. . . . And it's the farthest one. . . . This makes sense."

Now let's apply the four steps to the case we've just read.

1) *Skim the case study.*

In reading the case, we see that we're in a 9th-grade earth science class where the students are studying the solar system. The lesson covers two days. On the first day, the teacher presents basic information about the solar system—the planets, their relative sizes and distances from the sun, their orbital planes, how the earth revolves around the sun, the asteroids, and the paths of comets.

On the second day, the teacher begins the class by reviewing. Then much of the remainder of the lesson is devoted to a discussion of Pluto and why it may not have been an original member of the solar system. The teacher ends the class by having the students write a paragraph that compares how the earth and Pluto became members of the solar system.

2) *Carefully read the case, and make a written list of things the teacher or students did that you believe are significant.*

As we look at the case in detail we jot down items such as the following:

David takes a color transparency out of his file drawer.
David suspends a model of the solar system from the ceiling.
The students are given a chart.
David whirls athletic socks around his head.
David asks students to relate the demonstration to the model and transparency.
Mary Anne behaves as the sun and Kevin behaves as the earth.

David reviews by having the students work in pairs and write down as much as they can about the previous day's lesson.

The room becomes a buzz of voices and scratching on paper.

Randy drifts off.

David asks why Venus is called the Earth's twin.

Randy decides to take notes.

David emphasizes that students understand why events are true.

Juan says Pluto wasn't part of the original solar system.

David and the class discuss why Juan's statement may or may not be true.

David has the class write a paragraph that compares how the Earth and Pluto became members of the solar system.

David tells the students they should be finished by the end of the class period.

3) *Read the chapter, relating your list to the topics as you read.*
In reading the chapter we see that it begins by telling us that our information processing systems are composed of three locations where information is stored—the sensory registers, working/short-term memory and long-term memory—and a number of cognitive processes that move information from one storage area to another. As we continue we see that the chapter describes the characteristics of each storage area, noting that the sensory registers will hold a large amount of information for a very brief period of time, working memory will hold only a limited amount of information for a relatively short period of time, and long-term memory will hold information indefinitely if it is interrelated (in what are called networks and schemata).

In studying the characteristics of long-term memory we see that the chapter illustrates differences in the way Randy and Juan have stored information in their long-term memories; Juan's is more interrelated than is Randy's, and interrelated information is more meaningful to students than is information that exists in isolation. This suggests that the last three paragraphs of the case, which illustrate the ways the two boys think about their paragraphs, are significant. Because of better organization Juan had an easier time getting started than did Randy.

We then add "Randy thinks about his paragraph" and "Juan thinks about his paragraph" to our list and check them off.

As we continue our reading, we begin to study the cognitive processes that move the information from the sensory registers to working memory (and ultimately to long-term memory). From our reading we see that getting the learner's attention is the first step, which is followed by perception—the process of attaching meaning to what we see, hear, feel, taste, or smell. David's transparency, model, whirling socks, and the students acting as the sun and the earth were all attention getters, and David's materials were as concrete as he could make them, which helped the students accurately perceive the information that was presented. We check these items on our list, so it now appears as follows:

David takes a color transparency out of his file drawer.
✓ David suspends a model of the solar system from the ceiling
The students are given a chart.
✓ David whirls athletic socks around his head.
David asks students to relate demonstration to model and transparency.
✓ Mary Anne behaves as the sun and Kevin behaves as the earth
David reviews by having the students work in pairs and write down as much as they can about the previous day's lesson.
The room becomes a buzz of voices and scratching on paper.
Randy drifts off.
David asks why Venus is called the Earth's twin.
Randy decides to take notes.
David emphasizes that students understand why events are true.
Juan says Pluto wasn't part of the original solar system.
David and the class discuss why Juan's statement may or may not be true.
David has the class write a paragraph that compares how the Earth and Pluto became members of the solar system.

4

David tells the students they should be finished by the end of the class period.

✓ Randy thinks about his paragraph.
✓ Juan thinks about his paragraph.

As we read further, we see that learning is increased if new information is made meaningful by interrelating it and connecting it to information the students already know. Requiring the learners to be active instead of allowing them to sit passively also increases learning.

David's chart is way of helping students interrelate information by organizing it in a matrix, and asking the students to relate the demonstration to the model, reviewing the previous day's lesson, emphasizing that students understand why events are true, the discussion of whether or not Pluto was an original member of the solar system, and the assigned paragraphs further encourage the students to interrelate the information. Review also helps them connect new information to old, and the discussion and writing require the students to be active.

We check these additional items on our list, so it now appears as follows:

✓ David takes a color transparency out of his file drawer.
✓ David suspends a model of the solar system from the ceiling
✓✓ The students are given a chart.
✓ David whirls athletic socks around his head.
✓✓ David asks students to relate demonstration to model and transparency.
✓ Mary Anne behaves as the sun and Kevin behaves as the earth
✓✓ David reviews by having the students work in pairs and write down as much as they can about the previous day's lesson.
The room becomes a buzz of voices and scratching on paper.
Randy drifts off.
✓✓ David asks why Venus is called the Earth's twin.
Randy decides to take notes.
✓✓ David emphasizes that students understand why events are true.
✓✓ Juan says Pluto wasn't part of the original solar system.
✓✓ David and the class discuss why Juan's statement may or may not be true.
✓✓ David has the class write a paragraph that compares how the Earth and Pluto became members of the solar system.
David tells the students they should be finished by the end of the class period.
✓ Randy thinks about his paragraph.
✓ Juan thinks about his paragraph.

As we near the end of the chapter we see that students' awareness of and ability to control their cognitive processes also increases learning. This helps us understand the significance of *Randy drifting off* and later *deciding to take notes;* taking notes helped him control his attention. If we hadn't included these items on our original list, we would add them now.

4) *Examine unchecked items on the list.*
In examining our list, we see that we have only two items remaining: "The room becomes a buzz of voices and scratching on paper," and "David tells the students they should be finished by the end of the class period." These behaviors are significant in other contexts, such as classroom management (chapter 10) or effective teaching (chapter 12), but we see no discussion of noise level and teachers' use of time in this chapter where the focus is specifically on the learning process. For this reason they are less significant at this point than the processes and stores involved in information processing.

As you saw earlier, the focus in this supplement has been on the beginning-of-chapter cases. Those at the end of each chapter have their own sets of directed questions, and you will also have the benefit of studying the chapter before you do your analysis. For this reason we have focused on the cases at the beginning of the chapters in this part of the supplement.

Good luck in your analysis of cases.

Chapter 1

1.1:   Answers to this question will vary, but we have all had experiences as students where teachers described the procedures for a class or admonished a student for misbehaving (the manager role), used a clever demonstration to attract attention or encouraged us to work hard (the motivator role), presented content or involved us in discussions (the instructor role), and gave tests and quizzes (the evaluator role). For your class the instructor and evaluator roles are probably most important and the manager role is probably least important.

1.2:   While this answer is highly individual, research indicates that prospective teachers enter the profession for intrinsic rather than extrinsic rewards. These intrinsic rewards include enjoyment in working with people, helping students learn and dealing with academic content.

1.3:   Many examples exist. Some would include using interlocking cubes in groups of 10 to illustrate place value in elementary math, pushing objects across a desk to illustrate the concept *work* in science, conducting a simulation to illustrate the passage of law in American government, and having students describe objects and writing down their descriptions to illustrate *adjectives* in language arts.

1.4:   Intuitive research results are more common than nonintuitive results, which probably reflects a tendency in humans to expect the world to operate in a sensible and predictable way. The same is true in other professions as well. Many more research results in medicine, for example, are intuitive rather than nonintuitive.

1.5:   If the research base in teaching was complete, controversies would not exist. The research bases in other areas, while probably more advanced than the one in teaching, are far from complete. This is evidenced by the fact that controversies exist in these fields as well, and subsequent findings often conflict with earlier ones.

1.6:   David's attempt to ignore Andrea's misbehavior would be one example of using reinforcement theory to explain and predict Andrea's behavior. He was inferring that his attention was reinforcing her antics, and he tacitly predicted that if he ignored her (removed the reinforcer), the misbehavior would cease.

1.7:   The case studies in this text are intended to illustrate the content of the text, such as constructivism (chapter 2), encoding (chapter 7), effective teaching (chapter 12), and the other topics that are presented.

1.8:   While there are several good answers to this question, two solutions are described on page 15. One is to keep a box of very short pencils, give a student the shortest one possible and ask that it be returned. The second is to require a form of collateral, such as a belt in exchange for the pencil or other materials.

1.9:   For reading instruction, in which there is a common text and in which the focus is on simple reading skills, ordered turn taking might be effective. Also, first graders are more naive than are older students and are less likely to "tune out" when they know they won't be called on. Older students, in contrast, quickly learn to read the teacher's instructional patterns and will be less attentive if they know they will not be called on.

1.10: The danger is that students who have been called on will be less attentive knowing that they won't be called on for awhile. Shuffling the deck helps reduce the problem to a certain extent. However, the deck of cards is a cumbersome strategy at best. Expert teachers are able to monitor their students, and they call on students based on their judgment rather than an artificial device such as the cards.

1.11: The greatest benefits of one-to-one instruction are the ability to precisely determine how much the learner understands and to direct instruction at precisely that level. Also, the personalization involved in one-to-one instruction can be strongly motivating. While no form of group instruction can match the benefits of one-to-one, some strategies such as cooperative learning, peer tutoring, and the use of computers can approximate these benefits.

1.12: Both teachers were faced with the problem of making abstract ideas meaningful to students. Both responded by using concrete examples to illustrate these abstract ideas.

1.13: Reflection was demonstrated when she "fretted" over the fact that her students weren't learning an important idea, when she mentally tried and rejected different strategies and when she discussed the problem with other teachers. Many people mistakenly believe that creativity just "happens," but this is not the case. Artistry in teaching is the result of a great deal of effort, thought and reflection. The saying, "Creativity is 10% inspiration and 90% perspiration" illustrates this point.

1.14: The number of interactions in a typical classroom influences the human dimension in at least two ways. First, it forces teachers and students to be together, making human interaction an essential part of teaching. Second, and unfortunately, the numbers of students and the complexity of teaching requires that these interactions are often quite brief.

1.15: Because classes are filled with diverse learners, the already complex classroom environment is even more intricate, and some of the suggestions teachers are given won't apply to all learners. In order to accommodate these differences teachers must be flexible and adaptable, which require many decisions. The better informed we are about the teaching-learning process and the characteristics of our learners, the better able we will be to make informed decisions.

1.16: These three strategies relate most strongly to the human dimension of teaching. An attitude of acceptance and caring, positive expectations, and valuing all learners are human characteristics.

Chapter 2

2.1: Of the three factors—learning, experience and maturation—that influence development, learning is probably the one most influenced by schools, while maturation is probably the least. Sometimes schools take maturation into account by holding an immature child back a year before beginning kindergarten or first grade.

2.2: The maturation part of development involves her physical growth in size, strength and coordination. The experiential part involves her practice both in basketball and in other sports. The learning part involves specific techniques she learns, both from her brother and others.

2.3: The kindergarten teacher can address her students' need for equilibrium by leaving plans and directions to ensure that the class's regular routines and procedures are followed.

2.4: Students' schemata will vary depending on their experiences. Usually these include expecting the instructor to hand out a syllabus and explaining course goals, procedures and requirements. When our expectations aren't met, disequilibrium occurs and we adapt our schemata to accommodate the new experiences.

2.5:   *Equilibrium* is the concept that motivates us to accommodate schemata. If our schemata don't "work," we are motivated to change them to put our world back in order.

2.6:   When a child categorizes a whale as a fish, the whale is *assimilated* into a fish schema. Changing the whale and fish schemata to adapt to new knowledge about both involves *accommodation.*

2.7:   All growth depends on existing schemata. Students who have developed schemata for successfully dealing with academic work can bring these to bear on future academic tasks. The converse is also true. Pre-existing schemata are most useful in areas such as math where learning is cumulative.

2.8:   The best remedy for this situation is to take the students outside at different times of the day and measure the direction and length of the shadows their own bodies cast. The process could be simulated in the classroom by using an artificial light source, such as a strong flashlight.

2.9:   Many of Celena's students had schemata that did not allow them to assimilate the new concepts. To support the process of adaptation she showed them pictures that caused them to accommodate their schemata. Further information could then be assimilated into the new schemata.

2.10:   Piaget describes experience with the physical world and social interaction as causes of development. Play gives them experience and the opportunity for social interaction. This suggests that early childhood programs need to provide ample opportunities for "play."

2.11:   Many possible illustrations exist. The following represents one possibility: The child encounters a social problem—he sees a toy that he wants but another child has it. He says, "I know how to get that toy. I'll go up to him with another one and say, 'Want to play?'" If successful, the child will have assimilated the new situation into an old structure. If unsuccessful, the child may adapt and try a new strategy perhaps saying, "That didn't work. Maybe he will trade the one I have for that one."

2.12:   Vygotsky would disapprove of students working silently and in isolation. His theory stresses the importance of social interaction in learning. Classrooms that encourage students to dialogue and share ideas help facilitate cognitive growth.

2.13:   Jeff used the first three strategies in Table 2.1. He presented a sample problem to assess the students' backgrounds, he provided instructional assistance by walking students through the gerbil problem, and he provided Javier and Stewart with feedback on their efforts to solve his assigned problems. Jeff failed to increase student responsibility.

2.14:   First, observe them as they prepare for recess to see how well they do on their own. Then model the desired behaviors (using either yourself or a student) followed by letting them try to dress themselves, providing only as much assistance as necessary. Finally, see if they dress themselves without assistance.

2.15:   Learners able to ride a bicycle with either the help of training wheels or an adult running alongside to prevent them from falling are within the zone of proximal development. The training wheels or adult provide the scaffolding. Children able to ride on their own (without training wheels) are beyond the zone of proximal development.

2.16:   Movement up the ramp is continuous while movement up the stairs involves discrete movement. Another instance would be the difference between grade level and continuous progress through elementary schools. In the latter, students move through the curriculum at their own rate rather than moving from second to third grade, for example.

2.17:   Without object permanence the child will quickly turn her attention to something else. When the child acquires object permanence, she'll crawl or walk over and look behind the back, searching for the missing object.

2.18:   The practice is appropriate according to our understanding of cognitive development. Preoperational children are capable of concept learning, the concepts are concrete and they can be easily illustrated with tangible examples.

2.19:   Social interaction is probably most important for helping to reduce egocentrism. Through social interaction children are continually confronted with the fact that other people's ideas and views of the world are different from theirs.

2.20:   Concrete experiences are important for children at these stages of development. One possible strategy is guided "play" where the instructor encourages the child to count the coins, for example, then change the spacing, count the coins again, repeat the process, and compare the counts in each case.

2.21:   The child centers on either the height or the length of the clay, she is unable to *mentally record* the process of flattening the clay (nontransformation), she is unable to *mentally trace* the process of going from the flattened piece of clay back to the ball (irreversibility), and she doesn't question her own thinking (egocentrism). The combination of these factors leads her to conclude that the amounts are different.

2.22:   If persons were innately able to view the world from others' perspectives, then egocentrism would have to be a learned characteristic, and we would have to examine factors in people's environments that would cause them to become egocentric.

2.23:   Addition and subtraction are operations that can be readily illustrated with concrete objects (e.g. beans, sticks, etc.). In contrast, to understand percentage, such as taking 25% of 48, requires a mental link to "parts of 100," which requires abstract thinking. (The simple idea of percentage, such as shading 25 squares on a 100-square grid can easily be demonstrated, however.)

2.24:   A formal thinker would be systematic, such as rye, turkey, and American; rye, turkey, and Swiss; rye, turkey, cheddar; rye, ham, American; rye, ham, Swiss, etc. The concrete thinker would be less systematic, such as rye, turkey, American; whole wheat, ham, cheddar, etc.

2.25:   A developmental approach in science would start with the child's experience and use concrete objects to teach about the physical world. Karen Johnson's approach at the beginning of the chapter was developmental.

2.26:   In many cases students from high SES families have more experiences that result in school-related schemata than do low SES students. These include, for example, books, computers, family vacations, and trips to museums and zoos. These experiences provide conceptual "hooks" for in-school learning.

2.27:   Since the size of the blocks is the most perceptually obvious aspect of the system, students *center* on size rather than the balanced scale.

2.28:   A likely possibility is lack of direct experiences with shadows. Research suggests that background knowledge in the problem domain—proportional reasoning in this case—is a critical factor in successful problem solving.

2.29:   Initially, Tracey's students were at *equilibrium* and had a *schema* for heat, the essence of which was that it comes from coats and sweaters. They *centered* on the fact that they felt warmer with a coat on than off, and they *assimilated* these experiences into their schemata. Tracey disrupted their equilibrium with her experiments, and as a result, they had to adapt their schemata through the process of *accommodation,* finally concluding that instead of generating heat, coats and sweaters trapped heat.

2.30:   Just telling students that they are wrong doesn't provide them with the concrete experiences needed to construct new mental structures. Piaget would say that words are inadequate and ineffective in changing schemata. (Further, a verbal explanation probably wouldn't have made sense to the students, based on their experiences, so the explanation would likely have left their schemata unchanged.)

2.31:   One way to provide a concrete example of *population density* would be to move the students into a small area and then into a larger one. Then, mark off an area of the room, such as a chalk circle on the floor, and place different numbers of students in it.

2.32:   The teacher might put a large object into the beaker, such as a rock or brick and prompt the students to notice that the water level in the beaker went up. The rock is tangible and it would be easy for the students to understand that the rock "took up space." The teacher could also put the cup into the beaker sideways to demonstrate that the cup alone took up little space—the water level goes up only slightly—whereas the water level goes up significantly when the air is trapped in the cup.

2.33:   The best suggestion here is direct experience and active involvement of the students. For example, if a teacher were going to lecture about air taking up space, she would demonstrate the cup in the beaker as you saw described in the text. Then, ask the students a number of questions to check their understanding of the demonstration, and continue demonstrating and questioning when the students' answers indicate misconceptions.

2.34:   Information is input into our information processing systems through our senses. Information is stored as *schemata* in our memories. When existing programs (schemata) are inadequate to interpret new information then re-programming or *accommodation* occurs.

2.35:   Several other strategies that are effective in learning vocabulary include using the words in sentences, looking for Latin roots in the words, and having someone else quiz us. In general the most effective strategies are those that put the learner in the most active role.

2.36:   After Karen's demonstrations, her students' likely mental representations would be the idea of compactness—based on her squeezing the cotton in the cup, and the idea that density changes when mass remains constant while the volume changes.

2.37:   One of the most effective ways to teach cognitive strategies is through modeling followed by practice. For example if we wanted to teach students to rehearse information using flashcards, we might explain the strategy and tell how it is useful and then think aloud (talk out loud) while we are using the strategy ourselves. Then we could ask a student to try it out, thinking aloud as he or she practiced it, which would be followed by having the whole class practice.

2.38:   The advantage in avoiding ethical issues is that controversy is avoided. The disadvantage is that moral and ethical issues, such as fairness and respect, are impossible to avoid. The advantage in dealing with moral issues is that students learn to examine and understand their own sense of morality. The disadvantage is that discussing morals in classroom settings is often controversial.

2.39:   In the stage of external morality, rules exist outside the individual and receive their legitimacy from their being enforced by others. An egocentric child would view the rules as the same for everyone and would not think of them varying by person or situation. An egocentric learner has difficulty with autonomous morality, because it requires an understanding of morality as a reciprocal process of treating others as we would want to be treated and a willingness to look at the world from others' points of view. Flexibility, modeling and discussion of moral issues when they arise help students progress from one stage to the next.

2.40:   Some possibilities are dating ethics, dilemmas with friends and friendships, and honesty with parents. An increasingly prominent dilemma for schools is the issue of ability grouping. Advocates for high achievers argue that their learning is retarded when they are placed with low achievers, while advocates for low achievers argue that ability grouping is discriminatory.

2.41:   A Stage 1 argument would be that he'll get caught and fail the course. At this stage the consequences of the act determine whether it's good or bad. At Stage 2 a person might argue that it isn't in his own best interest to cheat; he gets nothing out of it by cheating. At the second stage the benefits to the person are the determining factors.

2.42:   A person reasoning at Stage 3 would say that everybody else is going 65, so it's okay for me to do the same. At Stage 4 a person would say that the law says 55, so I'm slowing down. I don't care what everyone else is doing.

2.43:   There isn't a clear answer to this question. Rights and the dignity of the individual reflect western values, which means its not a "universal" principle. Difficulty in answering questions such as this one is among the reasons Kohlberg deemphasized Stage 6 in his later work.

2.44:   Both theorists suggested that development proceeds in stages, that development is uneven and unique to individuals, that development is gradual and that once a level is attained the individual rarely regresses to a lower stage. Both focus on individuals' reasoning.

2.45:   A female student, focusing on interpersonal problem solving, might say, "How can we help Gary out? What does he need to know to do his assignment." A male student, depending on the level of development might give responses ranging from "I can't talk or I'll get caught" to "I can't talk because it's against the rules," to "I'll help you even though I'm not supposed to talk because you need to get going on your assignment. It doesn't make sense just to have you sit there."

2.46:   Effective moral dilemmas should provide students with a concrete incident, which involves real people dealing with real problems. These incidents are most effective if students can empathize with the people in the dilemma. The question of keeping the money is concrete, for example, and the students can personally relate to the issue.

2.47:   First, it is impossible to avoid dealing with some moral issues, such as cheating and appropriate treatment of others. Second, this position is similar to one which argues that schools should focus on academics and avoid other aspects of students' lives (such as psychosocial). This position ignores the child as a whole person and fails to promote development in these other important areas.

2.48:   As opposed to differences in motivation, Piaget's stages reflect differences in the way learners process information (e.g., perceptually vs. logically).

2.49:   Motivation is an important part of *both* theories of development. Motivation in Piaget's theory is driven by a need for equilibrium, the innate need for the world to "make sense."

2.50:   Effective kindergarten teachers structure their classrooms to allow maximum opportunities for exploration. There would be different centers or locations where students can manipulate objects, try on clothes and costumes and build things. In addition, initiative is encouraged by providing all students with responsibilities that share in the care of the room like feeding the fish, watering plants, and emptying wastebaskets.

2.51:   Work that is too easy doesn't provide necessary challenge, which detracts from the development of perseverance and industry. On the other hand, being consistently faced with work that is too difficult can leave students with a feeling of helplessness which also discourages industry.

2.52:   Report cards at the elementary level often have an effort component next to the grade. This component is designed to provide parents and students with feedback about industry. Also, a section on work habits is often included which gives additional information about industry. References to social comparisons would be missing.

2.53:   The answer to this question varies with the type of students. Academically-oriented students will be strongly influenced by the formal curriculum, whereas friends and extra-curricular activities are more powerful got others. Families still strongly influence all students.

2.54:   Schools are probably most successful at developing industry—at least for students who do well academically. To help develop initiative, teachers can recognize, encourage and reward students for going beyond basic requirements. Teachers can help with identity by relating the topics they teach to issues in the real world. Also, class discussions are effective methods for helping students develop views about themselves and their relationship to the world.

2.55:   Research suggests that drop-outs often feel "pushed out." They feel isolated, alienated and confused. They have low academic self-concepts due to poor performance. Successful approaches to preventing dropping out focus on both academic success and integration into the mainstream of school life.

Chapter 3

3.1:   This rule of thumb probably overestimates how long students will sit quietly if they're passively listening, but it underestimates how long they will stay involved if they're active. If teaching kindergartners, the amount of inactive listening time needs to be kept shorter than for older children; explanations must be shorter and more specific; and learning activities need to be varied more often. Even simple behaviors often need to be modeled for young children.

3.2:   The advantage of holding a student back is that children can develop at their own rate and are more likely to be ready for school when they begin. The disadvantage is that time alone does not prepare children for school; specific experiences are also necessary. The advantage in directly teaching readiness skills is that it focuses on the tasks and skills that are most critical. The disadvantage is that the child may not be developmentally ready for the tasks. An alternative to both is to have a flexible classroom that offers students a variety of tasks that challenge different developmental levels.

3.3:   *Area* and particularly *democracy* are abstract and concrete examples are hard prepare. The concept of *area* could be taught with small squares (such as square-inch pieces made from cardboard) that cover a certain surface. *Democracy* could be introduced with concrete experiences like role playing and making classroom decisions democratically.

3.4:   A language instruction program based on behaviorist principles would focus on specific learner behaviors which could be reinforced by the teacher. The accumulation of the behaviors would indicate language development. The teacher's role would be to structure the environment and provide reinforcement. The student's role would be to demonstrate the desired behaviors.

3.5:   Social learning theory provides the better explanation. The bilingual child hears both languages modeled and imitates them. Parents are unlikely to systematically reinforce both languages, which would be a behaviorist explanation for children learning both languages.

3.6:   A constructivist language learning activity would begin with some concrete experience, such as bringing in a pet. The pet and its care would be discussed, and during the discussion, the teacher would guide the learners' "active construction" of the language principles involved in the lesson.

3.7:   A child calling all men "Daddy" would be an example of overgeneralization. Children typically learn to discriminate through simple experience, but providing feedback ("No, that's not Daddy. It's just another man.") can accelerate the process.

3.8:   The nativist position best explains why virtually all children learn a language. Environmental theories, such as social learning theory best explain why some children have better language backgrounds than do others.

3.9:   Behaviorism would explain the development of dialects by suggesting that children are reinforced for speaking as they do by their parents and peers. Social learning theory would suggest that dialects are learned by observing the speech patterns of models and imitating them.

3.10:   A major disadvantage to the rejection-and-correction approach is that it pits the school against the child's home culture and also gives the child the feeling of being "wrong." The advantage is that it focuses on "standard English" and attempts to provide positive and negative examples. The advantage of the complete acceptance approach is that it builds on the child's existing language base and minimizes home-school differences. The disadvantage is that it might not provide models who speak standard English, which could be a disadvantage for the learner in later schooling or in the workplace.

3.11:   The teacher needs to approach language diversity positively—all languages are good and different languages allow us to learn about each other. Objects around the room could be labeled in different languages and students can be encouraged to learn from each other. Similarities and differences between languages could be compared and peer tutoring and cooperative learning could be used to bring different languages together.

3.12:   Maintenance programs attempt to maintain equilibrium by continuing the child's first language. A bilingual teacher can help students assimilate aspects of the new language by pointing out similarities between the two languages. Differences in vocabulary, sounds, and sentence structure will be accommodated as the result of forming new schemata.

3.13: Maintenance and transitional programs are similar in that they both build on the first language. The major difference is that maintenance programs attempt to retain the first language while transitional programs' main focus is on learning the second language. As world economies become more global, bilingualism will be increasingly valued, so maintenance programs will probably be preferable.

3.14: Successful immersion programs offer instruction within the zone of proximal development, allowing successful acquisition of the new language. Unsuccessful programs offer instruction that is outside the zone, not allowing students to benefit from the teaching.

3.15: An ESL program based on behaviorist principles would break instruction into discrete skills, the performance of which would be reinforced. A program based on social learning theory would be based on various forms of modeling, which students would be encouraged to imitate.

3.16: The great diversity found in most classrooms would argue against a single, monolithic approach. In addition, research suggests a flexible, adaptive approach which builds on existing language strengths. Teachers and administrators at the school and district level should have the freedom to apply research findings to their unique settings.

3.17: Several open-ended questions might include, "What do we have here?" "What do you see up here?" "What do you observe?" or "How might we describe what we see?" Then, responding to student answers, the teacher could promote language development with statements such as, "Yes, that is a leg bone. It's called a *femur*," and "Good observation! The head is surrounded by a bone. That's the *cranium*."

3.18: The whole language approach is compatible with both psycholinguistic and social learning theories of language acquisition. It builds on children's natural and innate need to communicate (a psycholinguistic view), and it stresses the natural use of language in social situations, affording opportunities to learn through modeling (a social learning view). Whole language is least compatible with behaviorist theories which stress the reinforcement of small, discrete responses.

3.19: Because the student is thinking in Spanish, the student is also speaking in Spanish. Ideally the teacher should write the Spanish down as it was spoken. This acknowledges the legitimacy of the child's spoken language and allows the child to see it in writing. The teacher might also call the child's attention to the fact that he or she is speaking and writing in two languages, developing the students' metalinguistic awareness.

3.20: A simple way of providing a concrete experience would be to write about a classroom event using the chalkboard or overhead. For example, following a field trip the teacher could invite students to help compose a story about the field trip. During the writing exercise the teacher could emphasize the need for capital letters and end of sentence punctuation.

3.21: Competition, with its emphasis on winners and losers has little place in the early school curriculum. Instead, the curriculum should emphasize mastery of basic skills for all, as well as cooperation and group cohesiveness.

3.22: The following might be an explanation for gender stereotyping: Historically, certain occupations and roles were seen in our society as "male" or "female," and students formed schemata based upon these experiences and their interactions with adults. Additional experiences are then assimilated into these schemata. Gender stereotyping can be changed by exposing students to non-traditional role models (e.g., women as carpenters and men as nurses), which requires accommodation of the original schemata.

3.23: Small group work, group projects, cooperative learning, peer tutoring and student-led discussions could all be used to promote social development.

3.24: An authoritarian style does not provide the freedom which children need to develop a sense of initiative. In contrast, a permissive style doesn't provide enough structure or challenge to develop student initiative. An authoritative style balances the other two, providing opportunities for both challenge and support which encourages the development of initiative.

3.25: While answers to this question are individual, permissive teachers often are less structured and less demanding. Some students react positively to this freedom while others resent the perceived lack of challenge. Authoritarian classrooms are rigidly structured. Again, some students are comfortable in this kind of environment, while others become resentful or even rebellious.

3.26: Piaget's emphasis on early experience and social interaction in promoting learner development have strongly influenced many early childhood programs, including *Head Start*. The influence has resulted in the emphasis on hands-on experiences and social skill development in these programs.

3.27: In addition to the specific information about buses students are learning how to attack a problem, gather information and work in groups. The only way to validly measure these goals is to put students into other situations and look for their abilities to solve new problems and cooperate. (Paper and pencil tests are inadequate to measure these goals, which is why we're seeing the present emphasis on "authentic" assessment.)

3.28: A direct instructional approach would specify the terminal behaviors and provide instruction to develop those behaviors. For example, a direct instruction approach might target "2" and "3" and begin by saying, "Three comes after two because three is more than two," and the instructor would then show the students an example, such as three sticks or counters compared to two sticks or counters. A developmental approach would place more emphasis on individual discovery when the child is "ready." Using this approach a teacher might set up a learning center where students would order a variety of objects and check their answers through self-correcting feedback.

3.29: Neither approach, per se, is necessarily better for language development. Both can be effective if opportunities to verbalize or "think aloud" while students are "working" on academic tasks. Teachers' questions like, "What do you do first?" and "Why did you do that?" encourage students to verbalize and think about their mental processes.

3.30: One possible explanation is that students who don't do well in school like to watch more television, which detracts from study time. Also, television makes children passive, robbing them of opportunities to read, play and actively explore their environment. Some teachers use television as a teaching tool, asking students to watch educational programs and having them write about the programs, or using television programs as themes for skits and plays. Also, television provides vicarious experiences, such as geographic specials, that are otherwise unavailable to students.

3.31: When concrete materials are used, teachers would likely talk less, but more significantly the kind of teacher talk changes. Instead of lecturing teachers guide students' thinking with questioning, which results in students explaining their thinking. This type of process provides a powerful foundation for continued cognitive growth.

3.32: Self concepts are the perceptions people have about their competence in each of the areas. For example, a skilled athlete would have a positive physical self-concept, a person who relates well to others would develop a positive social self-concept, and a high achiever would develop a positive academic self-concept. Our contacts with the world are powerful forces in shaping these different self-concepts. Schools, family, and peers all play a role in the development of self-concept.

3.33:   Any learning activity that provides students with feedback about their competence provides data that students can use in the formation of self-concept. The teacher can influence the impact of these data sources by stressing mastery of content versus competition, by designing activities that provide success, and by building classrooms where all students feel loved and accepted.

3.34:   The schools influence social and physical self-concepts through both formal and extra-curricular activities. In the classroom the teacher can involve students in activities that promote opportunities for student interaction and that develop healthy self-concepts. The teacher's management and evaluation systems are also important. Extra-curricular activities strongly influence the development of students' social and particularly physical self-concepts. Educators are divided on the relative emphasis schools should take in leading extra-curricular activities. Strict academicians contend the role should be minimal; others stress the importance of these activities for motivation and total development.

3.35:   The strongest effect is the influence of high achievement in improving self-concept. However, students with healthy self-concepts are often more motivated than their peers with lower self-concepts, so the process works both ways, at least to a certain extent.

3.36:   Grades are probably the most important school related influence on academic self concept, especially for older children. Students as early as first and second grade begin to understand their level of competence compared to others. Teachers can use grades constructively by having them reflect improvement and mastery of topics rather than performance compared to other students.

3.37:   Coregulation provides students with the opportunity to take initiative within the bounds of general rules and regulations. An authoritarian style with its emphasis on conformity to rigid rules would least promote initiative.

3.38:   Coregulation occurs when the teacher's influence affects student behavior; self-regulation occurs when students control their own behavior through internal control. Perhaps the best indicator of each is whether the teacher is physically present in the room. If students control their behavior with the teacher present, coregulation is occurring; if they behave in the absence of the teacher, self-regulation exists.

3.39:   The general pattern that emerges is that children may come to school with fewer of their personal needs being met. Whereas, specific curricular changes such as sex or drug education may be required, larger needs for developing self-regulated learners requires teaching orientations that focus on the development of healthy individuals.

3.40:   First, you could try to communicate that you care about him as a person by spending a few minutes with him periodically to talk about non-academic matters. Second, you could can involve him in learning activities that promote success, such as using concrete materials and open-ended questioning. Third, you can use cooperative activities in which he has the opportunity to interact with other students on an equal basis.

3.41:   The first thing you should do is seek professional help from your principal, school psychologist or school counselor, reporting your concerns and being specific about details.

3.42:   Child abuse and neglect would have adverse effects on development during each of these stages. It is devastating to a sense of trust, it elicits feelings of shame rather than autonomy, and an abused child is left strongly confused. Each of these leaves individuals ill equipped to give themselves over to another, resulting in a feeling of isolation.

3.43: The role that schools play in this process has changed over time, with current thinking placing a much greater emphasis on physical self awareness. Health classes are probably the most appropriate place, with health teachers being especially trained to deal with these issues. Teachers in all areas of the curriculum can communicate a positive message about physical diversity.

3.44: The answer to this question will vary according to individuals. Some will have feelings consistent with the findings of research, while others' feelings will differ somewhat.

3.45: The general pattern is that these health risks are greater for low SES youths. Teachers of these students need to make a special effort to address these problems in their teaching.

3.46: The changes in the American family provide extra challenges to youth, often resulting in increased experimentation with and dependence on drugs and alcohol. Schools are being asked to assume greater responsibilities for these problems. Businesses that hire these students are also facing the challenges of these problems and need policies and interventions to deal with them.

3.47: Though research is not entirely clear, general patterns exist. Students who fail to develop healthy self-concepts are prone to suicide, as are egocentric youths who tend to focus on their own problems rather than placing these problems in a larger perspective. The relationship between suicide and achievement is more complex; some high achieving students consumed with perfection and self-doubts attempt suicide, while other students who struggle with failure in school also attempt suicide.

3.48: Maria's students demonstrated systematic thinking when they attacked the pendulum problem in an organized way. First, they kept length constant and systematically varied the weight; then they kept the weight constant and systematically varied length.

3.49: Thinking out loud best relates to Vygotsky's concept of inner speech.

3.50: Schools do play a role in the social development of adolescents; schools and school-related activities provide the major arena in which social development occurs. In our opinion schools ought to take a conscious role in this important part of development. Strict academicians would argue that the primary role of schools is to teach kids to think and that social development is peripheral to the main goal of schools.

3.51: The following describe some rough generalizations: Early developing students are treated as mature and they become independent because of expectations. Career decisions are usually delayed, so they are not strongly influenced by physical development. Boys in particular tend to gravitate toward peers who are similar to themselves in physical development. Early developing girls would most likely face the challenges of sexual adjustment and different sex, peer-group relations earlier than both late developing girls and boys.

3.52: One theory is that the drop in self-concept is inevitable, the result of major physical and psychological changes that result in old identities being discarded and other ones adopted. A second view is that this drop is due to changes in schools, where students go from secure and personal elementary schools to large and impersonal junior highs. If the second view is correct, we can do more to make transitional schools more adaptive and accommodating.

3.53: In general, small towns and communities in which role expectations are clear and career paths are clearly defined provide easier paths to identity resolution. Whether these clearly defined paths are better in the long run is not clear.

3.54: American youth have the luxury of extended school, postponing clear career decisions into late adolescence and the early twenties. At the turn of the century most teenagers worked. Now over half go on to college and many delay choosing a career path until after four years of college.

3.55: Teachers can do much to minimize competition and ability grouping within their classrooms, and can also work to insure close and personalized contact with students and a curriculum that stresses student autonomy and problem solving. In addition, teachers can also help to shape school policies that influence larger issues like departmentalization and school size, such as helping to create schools within a school.

3.56: The teaching challenges are similar in that teachers at both levels must struggle with high numbers of students in attempting to create warm, nurturant environments that are conducive to personal, social and cognitive growth. They are different in that there is more emphasis on developmental changes at the junior high level.

Chapter 4

4.1: The practice of building on students' cultural backgrounds has two interrelated goals. One is to present new information so that existing schemata can assimilate it. The other is to present information in such a way that effective accommodation occurs, resulting in the creation of new schemata.

4.2: With the rapid changes that are occurring in our modern world, the capacity to acquire knowledge, or the ability to learn, is probably most important, because it influences our ability to adapt. While all three are very important, the ability to think and reason in the abstract is probably least important for most people. In a primitive nomadic culture, problem solving ability is most important followed by the capacity to acquire knowledge.

4.3: Experience strongly influences the capacity to acquire knowledge, because it provides background to which new information can be related. For example, people hear an educational psychology lecture that describes cognitive development; some have had an introductory psychology course and others haven't. Terms such as "cognitive" and "development" will be more meaningful for those with the additional background, and consequently they will acquire more knowledge.

4.4: The three dimensions of intelligence—abstract reasoning, problem solving and capacity to acquire knowledge—suggest different types of intelligence. As we'll see in Chapters 7 and 8 these dimensions are closely related.

4.5: Guilford's model would imply that intelligence tests should have a number of subtests (e.g., 120), and each of these would be reported separately to students. The large number of subtests has made Guilford's model cumbersome and impractical.

4.6: Most of the dimensions are dealt with at the elementary level and these are reflected in most elementary report cards. One exception is spatial intelligence. Two that might need explaining are interpersonal and intrapersonal intelligence. These are reflected in items such as, "Works well with others," and "Demonstrates self control" on elementary school report cards. Secondary schools are narrower in their emphasis, and courses and report cards are aligned with academic subjects like math, English and social studies.

4.7: The metacomponent might act first and ask questions such as, "What do I know about cars?" and "Where can I find more information about them?" The knowledge acquisition component would regulate the intake of information and organize it in a meaningful way. The performance component would involve the actual data gathering and driving from dealer to dealer.

4.8:   Most would argue that schools emphasize students adapting to the regular school curriculum, i.e., there is one "program" and students are expected to fit in. We would argue that schools should place more emphasis on changing the environment to fit students' needs. This might better prepare students to be life-long learners. Probably the least desirable goal is selecting out, but even this can be worthwhile if students learn from it (e.g., changing a major or transferring to another school).

4.9:   Sternberg's theory, like Piaget's, stresses that intelligence is modified through experience. Both relate old knowledge to new in the creation of patterns. Both suggest that schools should provide students with opportunities to examine new situations and relate them to what they already know.

4.10:   Sternberg's processing components are most similar to Spearman's "g". The other two components attempt to explain how intelligence relates to the environment and how it is modified by experience.

4.11:   Attempts to promote the growth of intelligence have included: 1) the kind and quality of experiences, such as trips to museums, the opportunity to work with manipulatives, and the chance to conduct their own experiments, and 2) the number and quality of verbal interactions, such as reading to children, talking with them, and giving them analogies to solve. In addition, we would put the students into problem solving situations in which they were required to solve real world problems. These attempts are based on current views of intelligence which emphasize the relationship between intelligence and experience.

4.12:   In single trait theories a single factor such as Spearman's "g" has been explained in terms of processing speed and efficiency—the faster the information is processed, the higher the intelligence. Time is also consistent with the "capacity to acquire knowledge" aspect in the general definition of intelligence—the more quickly a person learns, the more knowledge that can be acquired—and the knowledge acquisition component of Sternberg's theory.

4.13:   Strategy instruction is most congruent with Sternberg's theory. It has a specific knowledge acquisition component in its description of intelligence.

4.14:   Educational psychology classes are essentially homogeneously grouped. They represent relatively high ability and strongly motivated students who have graduated from high school and have been accepted in a college or university.

4.15:   Guilford and Gardner would probably prefer within-class ability grouping. First, they would oppose between-class ability grouping because it groups students on the basis of a narrow range of dimensions, such as verbal and math ability. Second, within-class ability grouping allows the teacher to observe all the characteristics of all the students and to be flexible and adaptable in forming and changing the groups.

4.16:   Probably the biggest reason for the lack of within-class grouping at the secondary level is the existence of tracks or between-class groups. Other possible factors include teachers' lack of training and large class sizes.

4.17:   Table 4.3 on page 160 of the text contains a number of suggestions including flexibility, quality of instruction and positive expectations. Of these we think that positive expectations are the most important because they lay a foundation for all other instructional efforts.

4.18:   Students in high groups might respond positively to the group per se, or the classroom environment might be more conducive to learning. Both could result in higher motivation and self-esteem. The opposite is true for lower ability groups.

4.19: Our advice would be to avoid ability group; the potential benefits to the high group do not outweigh the negative prospects for the low group. Further, the content of elementary science is not so cumulative or hierarchical that it would require ability grouping. Our arguments would remain the same at the sixth-grade level.

4.20: The children of poverty often come to school with some of their deficiency needs unmet, which leaves them less equipped to move on to growth needs.

4.21: Cultural experiences and money in the bank can be compared in at least two ways. First, both positive experiences and money accumulate. Second, experience makes new learning easier, and in a sense, behaves like interest on money. They differ, however, in that experiences are used as a basis for "constructing" understanding as we discussed in chapter 2. There is no analogous process with money in the bank.

4.22: This finding can be explained from both a cognitive and affective perspective. Cognitively, parents who have higher levels of education will talk to their children differently, using an enriched vocabulary and will be more likely to provide stimulating early experiences. Affectively, parents who have succeeded in school will have more positive attitudes towards schools, will value learning and these attitudes and values are transmitted to their children. Walberg (1991) calls the combination of these factors the "curriculum of the home."

4.23: While the answers to this question will vary, in general many of the cultural differences that travelers have trouble adjusting to are basic and fundamental, such as unwritten rules for communication (e.g., time pauses and proximity) gender differences (e.g., dress and status) and the way time is used. Adjusting can be difficult because they are taken for granted and are almost unconscious.

4.24: While this is an individual response, language is probably the most pronounced element of ethnicity. Others are cultural values that predisposes groups for learning. All ethnic factors have at least some effect on learning.

4.25: Other examples of voluntary minorities include European immigrants at the turn of the century and recent Cuban immigrants. An additional example of an involuntary minority might be the Chinese coolies who were brought here to work on the transcontinental railroads and who were forced by prejudice to live in "China Towns." Mexican Americans in the U.S. southwest sometimes fall in between these two categories. Some were forced to become U.S. citizens by the annexation of large parts of the southwest; others voluntarily came here seeking a new and better life.

4.26: The answers to these questions are individual, and they have powerful influences on achievement. Some related questions include: When did you know you were going to college? How were your parents' expectations communicated to you? What influence did your peers have on the process?

4.27: The concept of America as a "melting pot" is an antiquated idea of immigrant assimilation. All immigrant groups retained a certain amount of their native culture and in a sense "accommodated without assimilating." Minority role models are important to minority youth because they are living, positive examples that it is possible to succeed without losing their cultural heritage.

4.28: One suggestion would be to talk about time in a learning activity. This might help the children understand how time has different meanings in different settings and cultures, and it would help all students better understand both their culture and others' cultures. A second adjustment would be in the level of classroom activity; minimize quiet activities in which the students sit passively, instead designing learning activities that would allow all students to use their energies in productive ways.

4.29: For many Native Americans competition is a foolish characteristic of white American society. For example, they would not be inclined to compete for turns to respond in class, instead withdrawing and remaining quiet. Withdrawal from participation would be an example of Ogbu's concept of cultural inversion.

4.30: Possible introductory questions might include, "Tell me what you see," or "Describe what we have on the board," among others. Also, "How do these sentences compare?" or "How are these sentences alike?" are excellent. Questions such as these allow a wide variety of acceptable responses and provide a guaranteed-success, non-threatening invitation for students to participate in the lesson.

4.31: From this study we might infer that Chinese and Japanese parents place a higher value on schooling than do American parents. Whether or not you've observed differences in classmates depends on your experience.

4.32: Ogbu's concept of *cultural inversion* suggests that for some minorities school effort and achievement are white American characteristics and to try hard at school is inappropriate for them because these are characteristics of white Americans. Lack of effort then results in falling farther behind.

4.33: The advantages of learning about students' cultures can be explained from both cognitive and affective perspectives. Cognitively, it provides insights into the background experiences of our students, allowing us to use examples and relate ideas in ways that are meaningful to them. Affectively, it helps us to understand our students' motivations, allowing us to adjust our strategies to their values and interests.

4.34: First, find out as much as you can about them—where they were born, where they live, how they make a living, and what they do for recreation, for example. Then use this information in learning activities as specific, personalized examples of the topics you teach.

4.35: The answer to this question will vary among individuals. The controversy over Barbie dolls underscores the powerful influence of societal influences on young girls. Parents should be sensitive to the gender-related messages being delivered to their children.

4.36: The decline in gender-related differences is probably due to increased awareness of gender stereotyping and the emphasis being placed on gender equity.

4.37: An extreme nature position would attribute all gender differences to genetic influences; an extreme nurture position would credit these differences to learning and experience alone. Interactionists would acknowledge the influence of both.

4.38: As boys move into the junior high years, they begin to mature physically. This maturation coupled with a society that values initiative and competitiveness in boys may account for the increase in male-initiated contacts.

4.39: Teachers are products of the cultures they grew up in and may be unable to distance themselves from the values and beliefs that permeate those cultures. Also, classrooms are enormously busy and complex, and teachers often act "automatically" rather than stopping to think about and reflect on what they are doing.

4.40: Adolescence is a time when girls are struggling to figure out who they are as young women. In the absence of female role models in science and math, girls may conclude that these areas are not ones in which females can or should excel.

4.41:   Gender-related differences in math and science are probably wider with low SES students because these students may come from environments where more traditional roles for men and women are maintained and valued. This suggests that teachers of low SES students should make an extra effort to combat these tendencies.

4.42:   Probably the same factors that explain gender bias in classroom interaction patterns also apply here. One is that teachers are products of a gender-biased society and may not be sensitive to this problem. The other is that teaching is extremely complex, and teachers focus on more tangible factors, such as delivering instruction and managing student behavior.

4.43:   Your response to this question will reflect your view of schools as agents of social change. A conservative view would suggest something near or equal to parity. A more activist view would argue for greater participation rates in an attempt to compensate for past ills.

4.44:   Like individual differences in general, some differences in learning styles are probably genetically linked. Other influences probably include early learning history, and cultural and home environment.

4.45:   Gardner's Theory of Multiple Intelligences had two dimensions focusing on interpersonal and intrapersonal intelligences. These might explain why some students are better at reading social cues and why other students prefer working along.

4.46:   While a relationship is somewhat speculative, field-independent students are more analytical than field-dependent students and are perhaps more reflective.

4.47:   A possible goal might be to have students use longitude and latitude to find locations on a map. Learning activities aligned with this goal would provide students with practice performing this skill. Finally, evaluation activities would test them on the same skill, measuring their ability to use longitude and latitude to locate cities and other geographic features on a map.

4.48:   At risk children may not come from homes that value formal schooling to the extent that is found in their more advantaged counterparts. In addition, they may come to school with vocabularies and experiential backgrounds that aren't as rich as those of other students. See Tables 4.5, 4.6, and 4.7 for positive modifications that promote success for these students.

4.49:   In earlier times schooling was seen as a luxury, not a necessity for people who would work in factories and farms. Today in our technological society literacy is a necessity for economic survival. Given the increasing emphasis on technology, this trend is likely to continue and even increase.

4.50:   Effective schools are places that communicate positive expectations for success and that create environments where learning can occur. This is especially important for students who may not have a strong history of past school success.

4.51:   Some of the characteristics include high expectations and instructional support that focuses on student success. In addition, high impact teachers add a human component; they show students they care by taking an individual interest in students' lives.

4.52:   Answers to this answer will, of course, vary. Most likely, however, they showed an interest in you as a person and were willing to spend some of their time with you.

4.53:   Each of these maximizes opportunity for success and minimizes chances for failure. Success in turn increases motivation.

4.54: Again, answers to this question will vary. However, research indicates that the lack of challenge usually detracts from motivation and particularly from satisfaction with what has been learned.

Chapter 5

5.1: The advantages for mainstreaming are twofold: 1) the regular classroom provides an environment for the mainstreamed student that is better socially and academically than one in which the mainstreamed student is isolated, and 2) mainstreaming provides opportunities for regular students to learn about students with exceptionalities. A potential problem is the increased diversity in the classroom which places more demands on the teacher.

5.2: Some simple modifications could include smaller instructional steps, shorter assignments, and more opportunities for practice and feedback.

5.3: Parents can also provide valuable information about a student's strengths and weaknesses, as can other professionals working in the school—previous teachers, specialty teachers, such as those in music and physical education, counselors and school psychologists.

5.4: In the past a major obstacle to students with exceptionalities was exclusion; often these students were kept from the mainstream of educational life by separate programs. A related problem which still exists today is acceptance; these students were often neither well understood nor included into the social life of schools and classrooms.

5.5: The law requires that a placement test be given in a student's native language.

5.6: Research indicates that integration into the regular classroom benefits students with exceptionalities in each of these areas. Academic performance improves because of a higher quality instructional menu and interaction with other students. Self-concept can improve as a result of academic growth and interaction with other students on approximately "equal footing." Peer acceptance can be increased if the teacher models acceptance and encourages acceptance from the regular students.

5.7: The least restrictive environments (e.g., regular classroom with specially designed programs) will serve the most students while the more restrictive environments, such as a special day school or residential school, serve the smallest numbers. This means that you will likely have two or three students with exceptionalities in your class.

5.8: Mainstreaming and least restrictive environment are not synonymous. For mildly handicapped students mainstreaming is the least restrictive environment. However, for a moderately retarded student, the least restrictive environment is a self-contained special education class within the regular school (or another school in the district). The least restrictive environment varies with the kind and severity of the exceptionality.

5.9: The construction of an IEP must involve parents in the process, thus ensuring due process. A central focus of the IEP should be the identification of a least restrictive environment which could include mainstreaming.

5.10: Curriculum-based measurement would focus specifically on the skill of finding main ideas. For example, it might provide the students with several paragraphs and ask the students to identify the main idea in each. Armed with this information the teacher could then work with students to improve performance in this area. Curriculum-based measurement makes the teacher's job easier by providing better evaluation data for the teacher, which can lead to better instruction for the students.

5.11: Some explanations for the disproportionate number of boys and cultural minorities referred for special help include the following: One genetically-based explanation suggests that boys are born more active; another is that boys are born with more learning problems. An environmentally-based explanation asserts that boys are raised to be more active and aggressive. A third explanation focuses on a gender mismatch with schools; since most teachers are female they create "female-oriented" classrooms that don't meet the needs of male students.

Some explanations for disproportionate numbers of minorities referred for special help suggest that minority children come to school ill-prepared to learn because of lack of experience in school-related activities. Other explanations focus on mismatches between the culture of the home and the culture of the school.

5.12: Tests, quizzes and work samples give concrete indicators of a student's classroom performance. Curriculum based measurement provides the same kind of specific information about student performance.

5.13: The term *mentally retarded* has a negative connotation that can inappropriately influence people's perceptions and cause negative stereotyping. The term *intellectual handicap* more clearly describes the handicapping condition, and helps us remember that the handicap doesn't necessarily involve physical or social problems.

5.14: While the answer to this question is not cut-and-dried, adaptive behavior is probably most closely related to problem solving; adaptive behavior involves the capacity to cope under changing situations. Adaptive behavior is probably least related to abstract thinking and reasoning because most aspects of adaptation involve real world situations.

5.15: In each category learners are placed in environments where they can grow as much as their capabilities allow. Restrictions only exist to assure the well being of the learner.

5.16: Strategy training is most closely related to the capacity to acquire knowledge because it focuses on improving the ways students learn. Strategy training also focuses on problem solving to a certain extent, i.e., attempts have been made to teach students general problem solving strategies.

5.17: Answers to this question will, of course, vary. Often, students with specific learning disabilities do less well academically and have lower self-concepts than their peers. Students with learning disabilities most commonly cope by using a variety of study strategies.

5.18: Learning disabilities and intellectual handicaps are similar in that both are handicapping conditions that interfere with learning, both can result from a variety of causes, and they are related to some type of central nervous system dysfunction. They are different in that specific learning disabilities usually involve students with average intelligence or above and are limited to a specific area such as math or reading.

5.19: A "nature" explanation would suggest that males are genetically inclined to have this problem. An environmental explanation would contend that schools are not designed for the characteristics of boys. An interactionist position would say that boys *are* programmed to be more active and prone to attention problems but that schools do an inadequate job adapting to and working with these children.

5.20: The discrepancy model is based on the assumption that intelligence is average or above, an assumption not made with the intellectually handicapped.

5.21: Most of these adaptations could be used in a regular classroom. The teacher's role would be to suggest alternatives to students, help them learn each strategy through explanation and modeling, and provide a supportive environment for all students.

5.22: "More of degree than kind" means that teachers don't need to abandon their effective teaching practices in favor of qualitatively different strategies. In the Rosenberg study, students were given regular homework with adaptations. For example, homework was an extension of successfully completed seatwork, parents orally administered a nightly quiz, and parents confirmed the completion of the homework and quiz with their signature.

5.23: Both involve persistent, serious handicaps, and both handicaps interfere with school performance. The nature of the handicap is different for the two; learning disabilities are cognitive, while behavioral disorders involve inappropriate or undesirable behavior.

5.24: Extinction was used when Ms. Ellenon ignored Sara's crying. (Attending to Sara's crying reinforced her, and ignoring Sara's crying removed the reinforcers, which resulted in extinction.) Differential reinforcement involves rewarding desired behaviors. For example, Ms. Ellenon reinforced Sara's completion of the assignments by talking to her.

5.25: The major advantage for students is that greater emphasis will be placed on programs for students with exceptionalities. A potential problem is that a student with a behavioral disorder, for example, may not get the specialized support that he or she needs.
    The major advantage for regular classroom teachers is that they will get more help from resource teachers in adapting their instruction to meet the needs of students with exceptionalities. A potential disadvantage is that teachers might be faced with a greater degree of diversity in their classrooms without the specialized support needed to help them meet all the students' needs.

5.26: Physical impairments are similar to those already discussed in that they impede the student's ability to reach full potential in the regular classroom unless special help is provided. These handicaps are different in that the problem typically is not a general problem with the central nervous system or brain. Instead, it is a malfunctioning of the eyes, ears or speech organs.

5.27: Both Piaget and Vygotsky would support these adaptations. Piaget would probably stress the use of concrete materials to help build abstract concepts; Vygotsky would emphasize the embedding of abstract concepts in appropriate social support.

5.28: All teachers consider the visibility of instructional materials when they organize the room. Working with visually handicapped students requires special attention to this factor. Placing visually handicapped students near the front of the room is a first step. Other modifications include constant monitoring of instruction to insure that any visual materials can be seen or are translated into another mode (e.g., oral or tactile). Peer tutors and assistants can be also be invaluable.

5.29: As with visual impairments, teachers need to be sensitive to the special needs of these students. Placement is again a factor; students should be seated where they have the best chance of hearing or can read a teacher's lips. If a person who can communicate in sign language is not provided, the teacher should try to turn directly toward the student when speaking, to speak clearly and slowly, and to repeat student answers. Extra use of the chalkboard or overhead will also be helpful.

5.30: Although ultimately teachers must judge for themselves, the general answer is no—for two reasons. Different treatment can send the wrong message both to the student with a speech disorder and to classmates. The overall goal in working with these students should be to help them adjust to classroom life and life in general. Specific questions should be addressed to speech therapists.

5.31:   In general the definition of gifted/talented has broadened and been refined to meet the needs of more students. The general thrust has been a broadening of the category to fit students with special needs in different areas of giftedness. There has been a parallel thrust in working with students having learning or behavioral problems.

5.32:   Fluency is the ability to produce many solutions to a problem; a teacher might encourage fluency by brainstorming at the beginning of a discussion. Flexibility involves attacking a problem from new and unique perspectives; a teacher might encourage flexibility also through brainstorming or by using other sources for new ideas. Originality consists of generating ideas that are new and original; teachers can stimulate originality by using analogical reasoning (e.g., something is like something else) and by postponing the judging of ideas prematurely.

5.33:   The most important thing that teachers can do is to accept and value creativity in the classroom. This begins with an attitude of openness, which accepts and encourages unique and even "off the wall" ideas. The ways teachers respond to student answers and questions, the kinds of assignments teachers give, and the ways assignments are graded communicate the extent to which creativity is valued in a teacher's class.

5.34:   Teacher nomination probably has the greatest probability of including all three because teachers are in a unique position to observe motivation and creativity in the classroom. However, teachers often need special training to recognize creativity for what it is (rather than view it as an annoyance). Achievement and intelligence tests are probably least suited to capturing all three because of the narrow range of abilities tapped by these instruments.

5.35:   Probably the only characteristics tapped by IQ or achievement tests are verbal ability and flexible thinking, and even then, these tests have difficulty measuring flexibility. This suggests that test results, if used, should only be one part of the identification process.

5.36:   Curriculum compacting is most applicable in content areas that are fixed and linear, such as reading and math. In areas such as art, music, social studies and some aspects of science, all of which lack this structure, curriculum compacting would be less valuable.

5.37:   Both enrichment and acceleration attempt to adapt instruction to provide an environment in which gifted and talented students can best reach their full potential. This is similar to the goals of a least restrictive environment.

5.38:   Gifted and talented students have a wide variety of options at the college level. In addition to a huge number of majors, advanced placement programs allow students to "test out" of courses, and honors programs are specially designed to accommodate these students. Both acceleration (e.g., advance placement) and enrichment (e.g., challenging majors, independent studies, Saturday and summer supplemental programs, and mentoring programs) are common.

5.39:   Most of these behaviors are minor instructional modifications aimed at cognitive achievement. These include effective use of time and effective feedback. Warm academic climate increases motivation, and successful and effective classroom management increase both achievement and motivation. Students with exceptionalities need positive expectations for learning, a warm and orderly learning environment, and minor modifications in sound instructional practice.

5.40:   Setting goals prior to a lesson and summarizing information involve students in learning new reading strategies. Most of the others (e.g., introducing key concepts and creating study questions) could be adapted to place more responsibility on the students.

5.41:   The Regular Education Initiative is similar to mainstreaming in that it attempts to move help for students with exceptionalities into the regular classroom. It differs from mainstreaming in that it eliminates supplementary pullout programs and makes the instructional help more general rather than unique to each exceptionality.

5.42:   One of the most effective ways to teach cognitive strategies is through think-aloud modeling. For example, a teacher might ask students who have mastered this strategy to verbally describe what they are thinking as they attack a new list of words, or the teacher could role play the process. Each provides a model for the other students to imitate.

5.43:   The computer program would first present a list of spelling words to help diagnose the students' backgrounds. It would then present the words they didn't know a second time, a third, and as many times as necessary to help them reach mastery. Gradually, the computer would increase the pace of the process. The disadvantage of this approach is that it doesn't teach students how to use the strategy themselves.

5.44:   Computers can be effective in ensuring high success rates and providing effective feedback. The teacher must use time effectively and create a warm and orderly learning environment.

5.45:   The most positive benefit of mainstreaming may occur in regular students learning to live with and accept students having exceptionalities. To accomplish the benefit, however, the teacher must consciously work to change the attitudes and beliefs of regular students.

5.46:   In both areas the skills should be specifically identified, explained and modeled by the teacher or other students. Then the student must practice the skill and be given feedback by the teacher.

Chapter 6

6.1:   Any behaviors that are instinctive or reflexive would not be called learning. For example, infants instinctively suckle, and we all blink reflexively if something comes near our eyes.

6.2:   The two components of the question-answer sequence—Magna Carta and 1215—have not been presented together frequently enough to form a bond, so the question (stimulus) didn't elicit the response.

6.3:   The bedroom, which was initially a neutral stimulus, became a conditioned stimulus, eliciting a conditioned response—the warm, pleasant feeling. The bedroom became associated with positive unconditioned stimuli, such as being hugged and tucked into bed by parents.

6.4:   Classically conditioned responses are emotional or physiological and involuntary, while contiguous responses are neither emotional nor physiological and they *are* voluntary. Contiguous responses involve simple stimulus-response connections, while classical conditioning involves "learning" to respond to formerly neutral stimuli.

6.5:   Initially, school is a neutral stimulus. By becoming paired with anxiety-producing situations (unconditioned stimuli) in school, the school setting becomes a conditioned stimulus. The school setting then produces the conditioned responses—anxiety and illness.

6.6:   The unconditioned stimuli are your consistently warm, caring, and supportive mannerisms, which result in the unconditioned responses—comfort and emotions related to comfort—from the student. Your class (associated with your manner) becomes the conditioned stimulus, so that the student is comfortable (the conditioned response) in class.

6.7:   Punishment often produces negative emotions. If writing is used as a form of punishment, the writing process can become associated with prior punishing experiences. As a result, writing becomes a conditioned stimulus which produces negative emotions (conditioned responses) similar to the negative emotions produced by any punishing experience. Writing then becomes an aversive process.

6.8:   The author has had, in the past, unpleasant experiences in a dentist's office. These unpleasant experiences generalize to all dentists' offices but not to medical doctors' offices. There must be some cues in the medical offices that allow him to discriminate between dentists' offices and medical doctors' offices.

6.9:   Extinction will eventually occur if the song (the conditioned stimulus) is heard repeatedly without being paired with the positive experience (the unconditioned stimulus).

6.10:   From a strict behaviorist point of view, we would know that praise is not a positive reinforcer if the behavior being praised doesn't increase. Praise might not work if it's not valued by the student or if it comes from someone the student doesn't like. (When we introduce ideas such as "valued" and "like," we are moving beyond the context of strict behaviorism, since valuing and liking are not directly observable.)

6.11:   The undesirable situation we're in is having the headache. Taking aspirin makes the pain disappear, so the undesirable situation is removed, increasing the likelihood that we'll take aspirin the next time we have a headache.

6.12:   Primary reinforcers satisfy basic needs like hunger and thirst while secondary reinforcers are formed through association with primary reinforcers. Behaviorists would not consider enhanced self-esteem a primary reinforcer. (Strict behaviorists would not consider self-esteem at all.)

6.13:   When students get one job "out of the way," they are following the Premack Principle, allowing a more preferred activity to act as a reinforcer for a less preferred activity.

6.14:   Through classical conditioning, neutral stimuli such as schools, classrooms and teachers can become associated with the negative aspects of corporal punishment. These formerly neutral stimuli then become conditioned stimuli that also elicit unpleasant feelings similar to the unpleasant feelings resulting from the corporal punishment.

6.15:   Detention is designed to act as a punisher. Being allowed to talk or finish their homework during detention might be reinforcing for the student. If this is the case, the detention no longer works as a punisher.

6.16:   The test for any punishment or reinforcement system is whether or not it changes behavior in the desired direction. If sending students to the principal's office isn't reducing the disruptive behavior, it's not acting as a punisher.

6.17:   Punishment, such as saying no, can be effective in suppressing the undesired behavior but it doesn't teach alternate behaviors. The teacher might sit down with Kathy and discuss and even model alternative strategies (e.g., "Can I play with you?" or "I'll trade you my toy for yours.") which the teacher could then reinforce.

6.18:   In operant conditioning we are attempting to make the processes of generalization and discrimination voluntary processes, accomplished through practice and feedback that result in the desired behaviors. In contrast, generalization and discrimination in classical conditioning are involuntary emotional or physiological responses.

6.19:   Building upon this response, the teacher might say, "Not quite. *Sped* describes the action in the sentence. That makes it a verb. Now, what word describes how it sped?" This feedback is specific, immediate, linked to the student's response and provides corrective information.

6.20:   For praise to be effective, it must be perceived as valid, i.e., it reflects actual accomplishment. Public praise for trivial tasks is ineffective. In addition, the source of the praise must be valued, i.e., the teacher must be respected. Developmental factors also interact here, with young children generally being more accepting of both praise and criticism.

6.21:   Shaping involves the rewarding of approximations of the desired behavior. To get Felicia started on the assignment the teacher might try starting her out with one simple problem and reinforcing her first for effort on the problem, then for solving it, giving her a second problem and doing the same. Gradually, Felicia would have to do more than one problem to be reinforced and finally she would have to complete the assignment.

6.22:   Since the beeper going off depends on time, it is an interval schedule, and since it is unpredictable it is a variable interval schedule.

6.23:   Many teachers who use a deck of cars to ensure that they call on all the students equally and at random shuffle them periodically to produce a variable-ratio schedule. Telling students what you're doing increases this system's effectiveness.

6.24:   The testing situation (where pop quizzes are given) becomes associated with other testing situations that have induced anxiety, so the testing situation becomes a conditioned stimulus, with the anxiety being the conditioned response.

6.25:   Satiation occurs more quickly under a continuous reinforcement schedule. This suggests a form of intermittent reinforcement should be used. The beeper system illustrated in 6.22 would be one concrete example; not all of students' on-task behaviors are reinforced—only those that occur at the time the beeper "beeps."

6.26:   Initially math and writing are neutral stimuli. If they are used as punishers, the process (of doing math problems or writing) become associated with other punishers which have elicited negative emotional responses. Math and/or writing then become conditioned stimuli that produce negative emotions similar to those that have resulted from other punishers.

6.27:   In both classical and operant conditioning, extinction involves the disappearance of a behavior. In classical conditioning the conditioned response disappears if the conditioned stimulus occurs repeatedly in the absence of the unconditioned stimulus. In operant conditioning the behavior disappears if it isn't reinforced.

6.28:   Satiation, extinction, and punishment all involve the reduction or elimination of a behavior. Satiation results from overreinforcement, extinction (in an operant sense) from lack of reinforcement, and punishment from either being presented with something negative or having something positive being taken away.

6.29:   Initially, Dan couldn't respond to her question. Mrs. Knipe then used the question, "What do we know about the hedge?" as a cue to elicit a response from Dan which she could then reinforce.

6:30:   This is a false statement. People tend to imitate behaviors they observe in others regardless of whether or not the model is reinforced. Seeing the model reinforced enhances the impact on the observer through the process of vicarious conditioning.

6.31: This is a form of symbolic modeling, since the students are seeing a film or videotape of the speech rather than watching it directly.

6.32: This statement is true. As we found in 6.30, people imitate behaviors they observe in others regardless of whether or not the model is reinforced, but vicarious conditioning can only occur if the observer sees the model experience some consequence for his or her behavior.

6.33: Observational learning suggests that the teacher *should* publicly reprimand Shelley for throwing the pencil, explaining why the behavior is inappropriate and how it might be harmful. (This would serve as a vicarious punisher for the other students.) Other factors teachers should consider are possible emotional reactions to public reprimands, the impact on classroom climate, and Shelley's personal characteristics, together with the history of her behavior.

6.34: This is a form of direct modeling which produces a response facilitation effect. The students already know how to "persist," so they are not acquiring a new behavior, and we have no evidence that they are inhibited with respect to persisting. The teacher is "cueing" their persistence.

6.35: Based on observational learning we would expect the effect to be greater on Black Americans than on others because of perceived similarity.

6.36: Model status and reinforcement potency are indirectly related. Reinforcement is considered a direct cause of learning for behaviorists, and potent reinforcers are powerful in their ability to cause learning. A high status model has a greater effect on observers than does a low status model, but instead of directly causing learning, the effect is to motivate observers to imitate the model.

6.37: The teacher could simply tell the students what to look for, then present the modeled behavior and identify it for the students.

6.38: Since we are neither directly reinforced or punished by behaviors we observe on others, we must form mental representations of the behaviors in order to be affected by them. As soon as we begin to consider mental representations we move beyond the context of behaviorism and into the context of cognitive learning.

6.39: The pause serves as a cue, alerting all the students that they could be called on.

6.40: The children may chuckle, comment, or in some other way reinforce the parents for displaying the speech patterns.

6.41: Since confidence is a feeling or emotion, this is an emotional arousal effect. It is the result of direct modeling.

6.42: Mrs. Evans's caring manner, and Carlos's home environment were unconditioned stimuli to which Carlos responded instinctively with a feeling of comfort (an unconditioned response). Mrs. Evans's room became associated with her manner and Carlos's home environment, so her room became a conditioned stimulus to which Carlos also responded with a feeling of comfort (a conditioned response).

6.43: Since reinforcement is based on a predictable number of responses, it is a fixed ratio schedule.

6.44: Since Roberto hasn't been successful in the past, he hasn't been repeatedly reinforced for his efforts. Since he hasn't been reinforced, be feels he isn't good at math. (A strict behaviorist wouldn't consider factors such as how a person "feels.")

7.1:   The extent to which they were reinforced and the reinforcement schedule would determine how well they remembered the word pairs.

7.2:   Cognitive and behavioral theories both focus on learning and they both focus on stimuli and responses. They differ in their definition of learning—behaviorism describing learning as a change in behavior and cognitive theories defining learning as a change in learners' internal capacities which in turn can produce a change in behavior. Behaviorism focuses only on behavior, while cognitive psychology focuses on processes internal to the learner.

7.3:   The globe is intended as a miniature representation of the earth, similar in shape with the proportions of landforms and water represented on the globe similar to the earth's actual proportions. The model of the atom is only intended to help us visualize what we cannot directly observe. The information processing model is more like the model of the atom than like the globe.

7.4:   The lines represent the flow of information. Fewer lines between perception and working memory implies that some information is lost from the sensory registers if we don't attend to the stimuli.

7.5:   Though the sensory registers are virtually unlimited in capacity, if the incoming information isn't quickly processed—beginning with attention—it gets lost. Asking a second question without giving students time to process the first can result in one or both questions being lost from the sensory registers.

7.6:   2HEALTH has chunked seven bits of information into two; the number 2 and the word "health." Also, the word "health" is more meaningful than the six numbers 4 3 2 5 8 4. The combination of chunking and meaningfulness makes the number much easier to retrieve.

7.7:   High achievers tend to use more efficient processing strategies than do low achievers and would be more likely to process information by connecting it to information already existing in long-term memory. Low achievers are more likely to merely rehearse the information or simply forget it. The same differences exist with young and old learners—older learners possess and use more efficient processing strategies than do younger learners.

7.8:   Information in the sensory registers is not considered to be under conscious awareness. When we attend to the information and attach meaning to it through perception, it is moved to working memory.

7.9:   Our working memories have limited capacity. We use algebra skills to solve physics problems. The better algebra student will have more working memory space to devote to solving the physics problem than the weaker student will have, since more of the algebra skills are automatic for the better student.

7.10:   Many of the word meanings will be automatic for students with good vocabularies. This frees working memory space that can be focused on processing the information in the lecture.

7.11:   "Processing bottleneck" means that there are limits to the amount of information that students can process in working memory. If this limit is exceeded, the information is lost instead of being transferred into long-term memory. Teachers can help accommodate the bottleneck by: 1) presenting information in small chunks, 2) putting the students into an active role by questioning them and giving them practice exercises, and 3) using visual displays such as the chalkboard or overhead projector.

7.12:   Your identifying the bat represents procedural knowledge; your comment is declarative knowledge. Procedural knowledge is the ability to do something, a case of which is identifying an example of a concept. Declarative knowledge is the ability to describe learning in words.

7.13:   This is a true statement. We might, for example, learn the definition of an oxymoron (declarative knowledge) by memorizing it, and we still wouldn't be able to produce or identify an oxymoron (procedural knowledge). However, we could not intentionally produce something in the absence of some descriptions of what we intended to produce.

7.14:   There would be fewer (or no) interconnections between the different bits of information. The items of information would sit separately and in isolation.

7.15:   You would be relying more on schemata (which include networks as subsets). Your ability to teach the lesson uses procedural knowledge in the form of schemata.

7.16:   High SES students often have a richer background of school-related experiences than do low SES students. This background provides more available links to which new information can be attached.

7.17:   The most helpful (assuming there are similarities in the two problems) would be "How are these problems alike?" This encourages students to consider the problems in a larger framework (e.g., time-distance problems, or percent-mixture problems). The next most helpful would be "What is the first step?" This would encourage students to consider the problem from a problem-solving perspective. The least helpful would be the more abstract "How do we solve these problems" because it provides the least tangible links to existing schemata.

7.18:   An expert would have a larger background of both declarative and procedural knowledge than would a novice. The expert would be able to apply the implications of topics such as cognitive development or behaviorism to both curriculum development and instruction, while the novice's knowledge would be relatively inert. Connections and sample test items help you form relationships among the ideas you are studying, such as knowing the difference between applying positive and negative reinforcement to a situation. The connections and sample test items also help you learn to apply your understanding to classrooms. Application is a form of procedural knowledge.

7.19:   The term "active construction" relates to the discussion of *constructivism* in chapter 2. It means that learners actively construct understandings that makes sense to them rather than passively receive information presented by the teacher. David's guidance also illustrates the "zone of proximal development," the level of student understanding where they can benefit from teacher (or other students') assistance.

7.20:

	Similarities	Differences
SR & WM	Information retained briefly.	Information cannot be retained in SR; can be retained in WM through rehearsal. Information exists as "true" reality in SR; perceived reality in WM. Information is "unconscious" in SR; conscious in WM.
SR & LTM	Large capacity. Information is "unconscious."	Information retained briefly in SR; retained forever in LTM. Information exists as "true" reality in SR; perceived reality in LTM.
WM & LTM	Information exists as perceived reality.	WM has limited capacity and duration; both are unlimited for LTM. WM is conscious; LTM is unconscious.

7.21:   If students aren't attending, information isn't moved from the sensory registers into working memory, so attention is a necessary precondition for learning. However, if learners misperceive the information, or if the information is not encoded into long-term memory, learning doesn't take place even if the learners are initially attending.

7.22:   Other students, their clothes, their non-academic conversations, movement in the hall, activity outside the classroom, and even classroom displays not related to the lesson are all stimuli that are irrelevant or are stimuli that may detract from learning.

7.23:   Teacher animation and movement are forms of orienting stimuli that can focus students' attention on the lesson. Standing behind a podium or sitting are not effective attention getters.

7.24:   If emphasis is overused it could result in satiation and would no longer have the intended effect.

7.25:   "John, why do you think people are fascinated with the legends of King Arthur?" is a powerful emotional orienting stimuli for *John,* but is a clear signal to the rest of the class that they aren't being called on. The alternate sequence is more effective for the whole class. To demonstrate the effects on the students, a teacher might try the two options and then ask both John and the rest of the class how they felt in each case.

7.26:   The simplest way of checking student perceptions is by asking an open-ended question such as "What do you see?" "What do you notice?" or "Describe the information for us." The question is non-threatening and the students' responses will give you indicators of their perceptions.

7.27:   Experiences help us form rich networks and schemata. Each experience is either linked to an existing schema or helps form a new one. As our networks and schemata become more complex and interrelated we have more "hooks" that can be used to attach new information to old. This makes both learning and retrieval easier and more efficient.

7.28:   The loop is intended to help us visualize the process of retaining information in working memory through rehearsal.

7.29:   Rehearsal is irrelevant for processing information in the sensory registers. This is implied visually in the model—we see no connection between the sensory registers and rehearsal, but we see the rehearsal loop above working memory, and we see the line between working memory and long-term memory.

7.30:   You would provide brief practice episodes every day (rather than long practice sessions two or three times a week). You would also put the students in as active a role as possible, for example give them a fact (such as $8 \times 7 =$), and have them state the answer verbally or in writing (rather than read the answer).

7.31:   Encoding and rehearsal are similar in that they both are used to move information into long term memory. They are different in that encoding involves making connections to information that already exists in long-term memory while rehearsal can be used to get the information into long-term memory by rote memorization alone (resulting in inert knowledge). If rehearsed information is later connected to other information, such as math facts being used in problem solving, it then becomes encoded.

7.32:   Perception and encoding are strongly related. The way information is perceived is the way it is encoded. For example, if a frog is misperceived as a reptile, it will be encoded as a reptile.

7.33:   First, the teacher could have encouraged connections by encouraging students to paraphrase the information in their own words. Second, the teacher could have helped the students link the information to the real world with discussions of lava and volcanoes and the fact that mines become hotter the deeper in the earth they are.

7.34:   The lesson deals with information the students know rather than on something they're able to do, so it focuses on declarative knowledge. A propositional network describes the information better than does a schema. It is an organization of relatively static information.

7.35:   If students' prior understandings are inaccurate, the inaccurate information can hinder new learning. For example, if you began studying this book believing that negative reinforcement was a *decrease* in behavior, this idea would interfere with your understanding of reinforcement and punishment.

7.36:   If learners were passive, misconceptions wouldn't be a problem because their learning would depend on reinforcement for correct responses rather than depend on internal schemata. The adequacy of the reinforcers would determine the validity of students' "understanding."

7.37:   Lecture is more closely related to behaviorism. Lectures tacitly assume learners are passive, make little provision for the limitations of working memory, and assume that learners will encode the information as it was presented instead of actively making sense of it for themselves.

7.38:   This does not imply that the information is not organized. In fact, the information is well integrated into a larger schemata suggesting that all living things get their food from the environment.

7.39:   Either one of two types of open-ended questions would be an excellent way to begin. The first merely asks the students to describe the information in the chart and the second asks the students to make a comparison, such as "How would we compare the Italians' reasons for coming to those of the Chinese?"

7.40:   You could promote elaboration by having them compare different verbals in the context of sentences, and you could also have them produce examples of verbals (also in the context of sentences). Both situations would also put the students in an active mode.

7.41:   Charts, matrices and outlines serve as orienting stimuli when they are displayed. Because information in each is interrelated they also aid retrieval.

7.42:   Older students' long-term memories will contain more information, and the information will be more interrelated than it will be in younger children's long-term memories. Older students' long-term memories will also contain more metacognitive knowledge.

7.43:   A form of elaboration would exist through the process of generalization, for example, learners classifying shapes as squares regardless of their size or orientation.

7.44:   You would capitalize on elaboration by beginning the lesson with a review of direct objects and then linking indirect objects to them.

7.45:   Elaboration does not have to involve the addition of "new" information. It can also occur when additional relationships are formed between items of "old" information.

7.46:   To be most efficient the orators would select locations that provided visual links to different portions of the speech, such as a doorway when the speech had something to do with doors, passageways, or openings.

7.47:   Virtually all mnemonic devices are designed to help students memorize information. While memorizing some facts is necessary, thinking skills, problem solving and understanding concepts and the relationships among them is much more important in learning.

7.48:   It is adaptable to learning word pairs vs. word lists. The learning of word pairs (e.g., foreign language vocabulary or states and capitals) is more common in classrooms than learning lists.

7.49:   Embedded letter strategies embed the first letters of information to be remembered into a single "chunk." Once the word (e.g., HOMES) is remembered, the word serves as a retrieval cue for the specific words.

7.50:   This is an example of retroactive interference. Learning the new numbers reduced our ability to remember the old numbers "retroactively."

7.51:   When closely related concepts are taught together, the teacher can specifically focus on similarities and differences, particularly those learners are likely to confuse. This helps reduce interference.

7.52:   Meaningfulness describes the number of associations between ideas. More associations make retrieval easier.

7.53:   Both information and the context in which it exists are encoded into long-term memory. When placed in the same or similar context, the feeling or mood is retrieved. A behaviorist would explain the same phenomenon with classical conditioning.

7.54:   Inert knowledge is information that is not connected to other items in long-term memory. This makes retrieval more difficult.

7.55:   He might have begun by saying, "Scientists have discovered something unusual about the planets in our solar system. All of them revolve around our sun in a plane like this; all except for one—Pluto. Why do you think this might be the case? Today we're going to explore some possible explanations."

7.56: "Different schemata" is probably more accurate. Because students don't have elaborate school-related schemata doesn't mean that their schemata are not well developed.

7.57: The best environment is personal, of course. If you're typical, you were beyond elementary school when you figured this out.

7.58: Beside egocentricity, the concept of *centration* is also involved. The student is centering on the color and ignoring the shape.

7.59: Modeling, either by the teacher or by other students is one effective process. The teacher can interject her thoughts about communication during a discussion, and she can ask other students to do the same thing.

7.60: The teacher can model the process by displaying a list of words, and using a "think aloud" to illustrate her own metamemory. She would verbally describe and illustrate identifying the ones she already knows and setting them aside, writing—rather than merely reading—the ones she doesn't know, realizing that writing is a more active process, and rehearsing the words in frequent, short intervals.

7.61: Seven-year-olds are not likely to understand the limits of their memories. (So, you better tell your friend's son to write a note to his mother while you still have him on the line.) The research on metamemory suggests a ten-year-old is much more likely to do this without prompting.

Chapter 8

8.1: There is some fact learning, such as the name of the person who developed operant conditioning, a great deal of concept learning—*equilibrium, centration, negative reinforcement, specific learning disabilities,* and *working memory,* for example, are all concepts—some generalizations, such as "Learning is increased if teachers develop new topics in the context of prior learning," and problem solving, such as "Samantha is a third grade student who claims her homework assignments are too hard and so she won't start on them. What might the teacher do?"

8.2: The second process is preferable because it provides a context for the process. The disadvantage in this method is that it is time consuming and demanding for the teacher. The disadvantage in the first method is that the process is taught in the abstract and isolated from a meaningful context.

8.3: You would begin with specific examples, probably of declarative sentences. You would reinforce students for correctly punctuating them. You would then move to specific examples of interrogative sentences, again reinforcing students for correct responses, and then to exclamatory sentences following the same procedure.

8.4: Some concepts related to the information processing model in chapter 7 are: *sensory registers, working memory, long-term memory, attention, perception, rehearsal,* and *encoding,* among others. Some concepts from chapter 6 include: *negative reinforcement, removal punishment, satiation, fixed-interval reinforcement,* and *vicarious conditioning.*

8.5: Some concepts in each of these areas include: music—*pitch* and *rhythm;* art—*line* and *perspective;* physical education—*aerobic exercise* and *endurance.*

8.6: The characteristics of *adjective* are: modifies noun or pronoun. The characteristics of *conifer* are: needle-shaped leaves, exposed seeds, and resinous wood.

8.7: Concepts such as *impressionism* in art, *classicism* or *romanticism* in literature, and *culture* in social studies among a great many others have "fuzzy boundaries."

8.8: *Noun* should be easier to learn, because it has fewer characteristics—name of a person, place, or thing—and they are more concrete than are the characteristics of *culture*.

8.9: Negative examples only tell what the concept "is not," and don't give any information about what the concept "is." For this reason, positive examples should generally be presented first. A teacher might have a rationale for presenting negative examples first, however, such as using them to establish a context or to review, and this would be perfectly acceptable.

8.10: An adverb would generally be the best negative example because adjectives and adverbs are more likely to be confused than are adjectives and nouns or adjectives and verbs. Examples and nonexamples most closely relate to the process of encoding.

8.11: Superordinate Concept: parts of speech
Coordinate Concepts: noun, pronoun, adverb
Subordinate Concepts: number adjectives (e.g., a, an, few, many), size adjectives (e.g., big, small)

8.12: Definition: A part of speech that denotes being or action
Characteristics: Describes an action; describes a state of being
Examples: hug, run, am, was
Superordinate Concept: part of speech
Subordinate Concept: active and transitive
Coordinate Concept: noun, adjective

The primary difference in the analysis for younger compared to older learners would be in the choice of examples and nonexamples, with more concrete examples being chosen for younger learners.

8.13: You would begin by providing the students with a definition of adjectives, such as, "Adjectives are parts of speech that modify nouns and pronouns." You would then clarify terms in the definition, such as *parts of speech, modify, nouns,* and *pronouns.* This would be followed by a series of examples (ideally embedded in the context of a written passage). Finally, students would be given another passage in which they would identify examples of adjectives. Again, more concrete examples would be used with younger learners.

8.14:   While more than one network may be valid for the concept *operant conditioning,* a possible network might appear as follows:

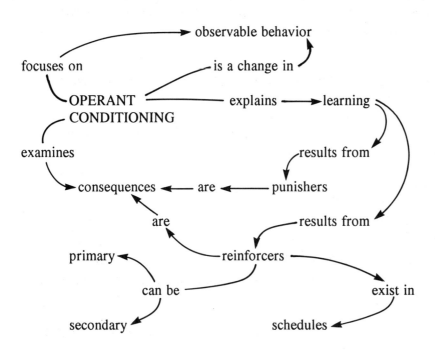

8.15:   This statement would be a generalization because it describes a pattern that relates praise to increase in behavior. It isn't a principle, however, because there are exceptions to the pattern. It summarizes a variety of instances where praise is used by teachers which are followed by increases in student behavior.

8:16:   Principles, generalizations and rules all describe patterns and can be used as a basis for explaining and predicting. Principles and generalizations are descriptions of patterns observed in the real world whereas rules are patterns arbitrarily derived by humankind.

8.17:   The best example would one that illustrates the rule and at the same time places it in a passage or paragraph to provide context for the use of the rule. A portion of a passage appears as follows:

> We all live in a *city.* Some *cities* are large while others are medium sized or even small. Andre, a small *boy,* grew up on a *berry* farm outside a *city* in France. He helped his father harvest the huge numbers of *berries* that the farm produced each year. Andre, like many of the *boys* who worked on the farms would hold a *tray* on which the *berries* were put. As Andre grew he often held two *trays* at once.

8.18:   We would provide specific, concrete examples, such as pushing on a wall and pulling on a doorknob. We would simply tell the students the name, and they would practice it through rehearsal.

8.19:   Social studies more strongly addresses the cultural literacy aspect of declarative knowledge than does math, because it describes our historical and cultural heritage.

8.20:   The simplest way of illustrating these concepts would be to find examples on students' bodies, such as, "When you have a sore throat often your glands on either side of your throat are swollen. Reach up under your chin near your neck and see what you feel," and "Reach down behind your foot. That 'ropey' thing attached to both your calf muscle and heel bone is a tendon."

8.21:   Other materials can be attached to the Velcro, just as new information can be attached to old. In the case with tendons, for example, once learners understand what tendons are by identifying their Achilles Tendon, they can use this understanding to identify other tendons on their bodies and also understand how tendons are different from ligaments and cartilage. The Velcro metaphor doesn't adequately explain cases where no connection between old and new learning is made.

8.22:   Some possible items might be:
1) Identify three examples of reptiles and two examples of animals that look like reptiles but are not.
2) Number a paper from one to five. I am going to show you a series of pictures. If the picture I show you is a reptile, write yes on your paper; if it isn't a reptile, write no.
3) Which of the following statements are true of reptiles?
   a. They are slimy.
   b. They have no bones.
   c. Some of them are covered by shells.
   d. They have scaly skin.
   e. They are cold blooded.

A writing assignment might be the following:
Select a reptile and write a paragraph about it. In the paragraph describe how the reptile looks, and how the reptile would feel if you held it.

8.23:   Changing ideas disrupts entire schemata. Retaining misconceptions allows learners to remain at *equilibrium*.

8.24:   Before her experience a network for Pam's understanding may have appeared as:

wet — reptiles — slimy

After the experience the network may have looked like the following:

dry — reptiles — smooth
                   |
                clean

8.25:   Cognitive strategies are stored in long-term memory, as are all forms of knowledge. No other place in the model provides for long-term storage.

8.26:   Patty's students were learning to take a complex geometric shape and break it down into simple shapes, for which area formulas were known. The process could be applied in a variety of areas. For example, in social studies students could examine a region of the world in parts, such as the climate, geography, and system of government in studying different countries' economic development.

8.27:   Jamey lacked two kinds of knowledge that Bettina possessed. First, he had a misconception about finding the area of a parallelogram, and he lacked metacognitive knowledge that would lead him to assess his own thinking.

8.28:   The second goal is more effective. It is short-term, quantitative, and specific. While getting a B is specific, it is longer term and qualitative.

8.29:   Study skills and schemata are related but not identical. Study skills are a type of schemata as are concepts, generalizations, and rules. Schemata are superordinate to study skills.

8.30: Answering the questions would be called a strategy, because they go beyond the normal reading processes used to understand the material. Answering them would also be called a study skill because they are designed to increase comprehension of written materials. All study skills are strategies, but not all strategies are study skills. For example, thinking skills are strategies but not study skills, and strategies exist in other areas, such as solving math problems.

8.31: Identifying additional examples is the best strategy, because it puts you in the most active role. Underlining the concept and its definition is the least effective, because it puts you in the least active role, and it also requires the least amount of decision making on your part.

8.32: Finding and underlining the key sentence is the better strategy because it requires a decision, which puts the learner in a more active role. Underlining the first sentence eliminates the decision.

8.33: Note taking is generally better because it is a more active process than underlining, requiring students to not only be selective about the information they study but also to transform it into their own words or ideas.

8.34: Summarizing requires the most effort and underlining requires the least. Summarizing is probably the least popular because of the effort required.

8.35: A simple spatial representation might appear as follows:

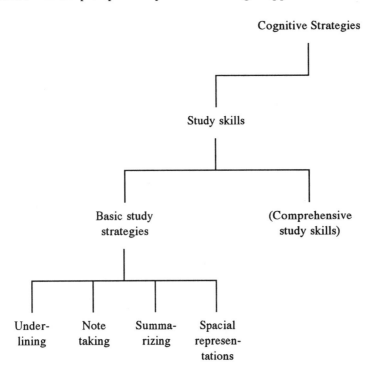

8.36: While beneficial to both, the strategy should be most helpful in study DNA. Constructing questions, trying to relate DNA to other topics in biology, answering questions about DNA and restudying difficult material should all aid a learner's understanding of the topic.

8.37: MURDER should be more effective. Processes such as paraphrasing content, trying to apply information, and analyzing errors on quizzes—all parts of MURDER—put learners into a more active role than they would be in using SQ4R.

8.38:   Reciprocal teaching has two additional elements lacking in the other two strategies. The first is the modeling and practice used to learn the strategy, and the second is predicting, which is another way of putting learners into an active role.

8.39:   1) Summarize—"Let's see, what would be a sentence that summarizes the paragraph?" 2) Construct Test Question—"Now I need a good question." 3) Clarify—"Are there any ideas in the paragraph that aren't clear?" 4) Predict—"Now, what will the next paragraph be about?"

8.40:   Reciprocal teaching, with its requirements to summarize, construct a test question and predict, probably requires the most active involvement. SQ4R is the strategy that requires the least involvement.

8.41:   This question asks students to confirm a conclusion with facts, a subcomponent of thinking critically.

8.42:   The answer to this question isn't cut and dried, because it depends on the topic being studied. However, in general, preoperational learners could use any processes that are essentially perceptual, such as recalling, recognizing, comparing and contrasting, and classifying. They can also infer, predict, and confirm conclusions with facts if concrete ideas are involved, such as, "We know that animal is a mammal because it is warm and furry." In addition to the processes already identified, concrete thinkers can hypothesize, identify relevant and irrelevant information, and check consistency. Critical thinking skills such as identifying bias, stereotypes, and unstated assumptions are abstract and require formal thinking. The ability to recognize over- or undergeneralizing depends on the topic.

8.43:   In questioning whether all marsupials have powerful hind legs, the student is recognizing an overgeneralization.

8.44:   The "domain" for this text is educational psychology, an area of psychology applied to problems of learning and teaching.

8.45:   Realizing that you don't know what the last three paragraphs said and rereading the material would be a type of metacognition we could call metacomprehension—knowing if you're comprehending what you're reading and being able to do something about it. Metacognition is less well developed in young children, so a second grader would be less likely to behave the way you did. Metacognitive knowledge is stored in long-term memory.

8.46:   Attitude would be best indicated by a person's inclination to study math beyond the requirements set by the teacher. The inclination to use a thinking skill without being prompted to do so would be the best indicator of a person's attitude toward it.

8.47:   Attitudes/dispositions and motivation are closely related but they're not identical. Motivation energizes a person to take some action (such as trying to understand a topic compared to merely getting an answer). In comparison, a person could have a positive attitude toward something without being energized to take some action.

8.48:   In real life, open-ended problem solving is more common. Real life problems are often unstructured, one best answer often doesn't exist, and the application of information from multiple disciplines is required. Students should probably spend more time in schools learning to deal with this type of problem solving.

8.49: The lemonade problem requires logic, but it is concrete, specific, and can be represented pictorially, so it could be solved by concrete operational learners if they have been given experiences with problems of this sort. (This would be difficult for many fifth and sixth graders, however, because they aren't typically given enough experience in solving this type of problem.)

8.50: The teacher could ask questions or pose problems that would help learners see new relationships or connections between old ideas, and thereby the students' "expertise" would be increased.

8.51: More interrelated schemata and the ability to apply the information in unique situations are two characteristics of expertise. Helping students find links by comparing related topics and requiring students to use their understanding in problem solving situations would both increase expertise.

8.52: The students decided to find the area of the school grounds—first by measuring the grounds, then breaking the area into simple geometric shapes, and finally adding the areas. They then found the number of acres and multiplied the result by the cost per acre. The students needed to know how to find the areas of familiar geometric figures and how many square feet there were in an acre, in addition to basic skills in math.

8.53: Devising a plan is *part* of a strategy. The goal is to solve the problem. Devising a plan—alone—won't reach the goal.

8.54: You could draw the six jugs and show each being two-thirds full. Then ask a series of specific questions that would require the boy to reconsider his thinking, such as, "Based on what we see, how much in two jugs?" "In three?" "Must we have more or less than six pints altogether?" and "How do we know?"

8.55: Understanding the problem is usually easier in a convergent problem solving situation. There it involves identifying a problem type, such as, "Oh yeah, this is a profit problem. I have to subtract expenses from income." A problem "type" often doesn't exist for open-ended problem solving, and the students' first task is to define the problem.

8.56: Learners would have to know the characteristics of voters in general and the kinds of issues that most interest them. Then they would have to understand some characteristics of people's motivation, which they would try to apply to increase the voter turnout.

8.57: *Networks* and *schemata* are concepts superordinate to each of these forms of learning. Each of these forms of learning are types of *schemata,* and declarative knowledge about the forms of learning is organized in networks. They are all stored in long-term memory.

8.58: These are both types of specific transfer. Even though the topics vary, the processes involved in punctuating are the same.

8.59: Adding the pencils and candy is also a type of specific transfer. The teacher could help the process by having the students solve a wide variety of problems.

8.60: Transfer is more likely to occur for a learner whose schemata are elaborate with many connections; elaborated schemata provide more access points and more connections between ideas.

8.61: An example that expands on the one in Connection 8.17 could be used. The passage provides context, and its quality is high because learners can observe singular and plural instances in the passage. It would need to be expanded to provide adequate variety, such as *y* preceded by *e, i,* and *u,* in addition to *a* and *o,* and a variety of consonants preceding the *y.*

8.62:   Transfer is more likely using a method such as Patty's. The alternative has students solving problems in the abstract and out of context. This results in less meaningful learning with fewer connections, which in turn makes transfer less likely.

8.63:   Though both forms of problem solving depend on domain specific knowledge, open-ended problem solving would transfer more broadly because it spans many disciplines while convergent problem solving is in a specific content area.

8.64:   The problem is a matter of emphasis. One teacher emphasizes fact learning and knowing information in a particular order, another emphasizes comprehension of written material, and a third focuses on problem solving. Communication among the teachers is a key to solving the problem. They could agree on some study skills goals and emphasize those goals across content areas.

8.65:   As with other forms of transfer, transfer of thinking skills increases if learners have an opportunity to practice the skills in a variety of areas, and if the practice is done in the context of realistic situations.

8.66:   Inert knowledge is stored in isolated pockets in long-term memory; movement of ideas between pockets is minimal. Generative knowledge is stored in interrelated networks and schemata.

8.67:   As emphasized in the chapter, the key to meaningful concept learning is a variety of high quality examples presented in context. If this is accomplished, the problem of inert knowledge will be reduced.

8.68:   In general, constructivists would be critical of Ausubel's views, particularly in his emphasis on expository presentation, because it often allows learners to remain passive. If a teacher promotes high levels of teacher-student and student-student interaction which allows learners to construct learning that makes sense to them, Ausubel's views and constructivism are not inconsistent.

8.69:   A possible advance organizer might be the following:

Transfer is like a formula or recipe we use—every time we use it the situation is different but we perform basically the same steps.

8.70:   Using a hierarchy doesn't necessarily mean that you must follow a deductive sequence. You could begin by analyzing examples and then use the hierarchy at the end to tie ideas together and organize the lesson.

8.71:   Tom put the examples of *hyperbole* in the context of a short written passage, and Patty put her study of areas of irregular figures in the context of the school grounds problem. They both illustrate the theme that "meaningful learning cannot be separated from the context in which it is learned."

8.72:   Students "discover" the idea the teacher wants them to understand, such as a concept, principle, generalization, or rule. The students must be provided with information—such as examples of concepts—in order for discovery lessons to work.

8.73:   The lesson might be structured as follows: 1) A definition of *hyperbole* could be used as an advance organizer. 2) A deductive sequence would describe *hyperbole* as a figure of speech, then define *hyperbole* and then illustrate it with examples. 3) The teacher would use an expository method to present the information in finished form, meaning the teacher would present a clear definition and the teacher would present the examples and nonexamples rather than guide the students to their own understanding. 4) As each of the examples are presented they would be linked to the definition and compared and contrasted with other examples and nonexamples.

8.74:   Patty's lesson more closely followed Bruner's ideas than Ausubel's. She started with a problem, and the students were led to "discover" the strategy for finding the areas of irregular plane figures.

8.75:   ·When guided discovery is used, teachers have goals clearly in mind, and they provide enough guidance to be sure students reach the goals. For example, Tom Fleming presented clear examples of *hyperbole* in his passage, which also included a nonexample (a metaphor). Tom then guided the students into identifying the characteristics of *hyperbole*.

Chapter 9

9.1:   At one point in the lesson Joe interrupted, interfering with Nikki's opportunity to respond. Classrooms need to be safe environments in which students feel secure to learn. Classroom management helps accomplish this.

9.2:   During the elementary grades students are faced with the psychosocial challenge of developing a sense of industry. The resolution of the industry vs. inferiority crisis has both short term and long term consequences.

9.3:   Punishment per se is not a motivator, since punishment reduces rather than increases behavior. The threat of punishment, however, can be a motivator, because a behavior can be increased in order to avoid the punisher—such as the example in chapter 6 where the teacher tried to increase appropriate behavior by threatening to take some of the students' lunch period away if they didn't behave appropriately.

9.4:   Consumables, adult approval, privilege and responsibility, and entertainment are all commonly used with young children. In contrast, older children respond more positively to independence, peer approval and competition—if it doesn't reflect on their ability. In general, the reinforcers in Table 9.2 are more effective with younger children. Older students are more influenced by their own perceptions and beliefs, are more likely to consider factors like the teachers' motives, and they question whether or not they're being manipulated more than younger students do.

9.5:   First, because of their tendency to be egocentric and to center, preoperational learners tend to focus on reinforcers—such as praise—that are directed to them and do not consider others. Further, because of their tendency to be perceptually dominated, they are unlikely to assess the sincerity or validity of the praise. (Also, assessing sincerity and validity requires more abstract thinking than is characteristic of preoperational learners.)

9.6:   *Shaping* uses reinforcers for successive approximations of a desired behavior. Students might first be given points, tokens, or some other reinforcers for merely turning in assignments, then a certain percentage correct would be required for earning the points, and finally the homework would be scored in a traditional way.

9.7:   When rewards are given, the tendency is for learners to shift their efforts away from the activity per se and toward working for the reward. Since no reward is available for choosing a particular free-time activity, their inclination to choose the activity decreases. Choosing easier problems makes sense, since learners are more likely to get correct solutions for them, which increases the likelihood of getting a reward.

9.8:   The teacher might have explained how all knowledge is interconnected and that the purpose of the AP class is not just to pass the test but to learn important information about the subject. (Speaking strictly pragmatically, the teacher might also have said simply and evenly, "Of course. Everything in this class is on the test." Then put it on a test.)

9.9:   Identifying punishers and reinforcers is simple. If the behavior being praised *decreases,* praise is a punisher; if the behavior increases, the praise is a reinforcer.

9.10:   The humanistic orientation is much more like cognitive psychology, because the focus is on responses to internal needs with both. Behaviorism focuses on responses to external experiences.

9.11:   Answering the question from a humanistic perspective, a teacher might say, "You'll be surprised. You get to where you really understand this stuff, and you'll be amazed at how good you feel about it. Then, when you can use what you've learned in your own writing, and you see the progress you've made you'll feel even better. I guarantee it."
        A behaviorist, basing instruction on a hierarchical sequence composed of specific, reinforceable behaviors, would say that we need to understand parts of speech, because our ability to write depends first on a clear understanding of the specific parts of speech.

9.12:   By noticing that Jennifer had been a little quiet and asking her to move into the middle of the room, Kathy demonstrated sensitivity to Jennifer as a person. Even if Kathy misperceived Jennifer's behavior, she communicated an attitude of concern for Jennifer and her feelings. Kathy promoted a positive climate in at least two ways. First, she tried to include as many students as possible in the activity by called on several of them by name. Second, she protected individuals' rights to be heard by admonishing Joe when he interrupted Nikki.

9.13:   The child is responding to his need for equilibrium. If the story sounds the same, he remains at equilibrium. If is sounds different, his equilibrium is disrupted, and he is motivated to reestablish it. Hearing the story as it has always been read is the easiest way to remain at equilibrium.

9.14:   According to Piaget, people are inclined to practice their developing schemata, and feedback gives them information about the adequacy of schemata. If they get no feedback, they're left with the uncertainty of not knowing whether their schemata are adequate or not.

9.15:   The interaction between behaviors and the environment is behaviorist. Attention and perception are two examples of cognitions (as are elaboration, organization, and all forms of metacognition).

9.16:   People tend not to value success on trivial tasks. If the value component is zero, self-efficacy is zero since the relationship is expectancy *times* value.

9.17:   After succeeding on any challenging task, you could communicate, both verbally and nonverbally, the pleasure you feel in your accomplishment. Because they could identify with it personally, an ideal situation would be describing the pleasure of helping your students understand a topic they previously didn't "get."

9.18:   The first might have thoughts such as, "I know I can get this. Let's see . . . what am I doing wrong. This problem can't be that tough." The second student would be more likely to have thoughts such as, "This problem is impossible. I'll never get it. Why do we have problems like this anyway?"

9.19:   The environmental influence is Mrs. Cossey's specific behaviors, such as doing the problem and/or praising Darren for minimal effort. Cognitions would be Darren's perceptions of why Mrs. Cossey behaved the way she did, and his perceptions of his ability to do the problem on his own.

9.20:   A number of possibilities exist. The following is one example: You could create a system where they had a worksheet with a number of facts on it, such as $8 + 6 = $ ___ , and they see how many they could respond correctly to in a minute, for example. They could then try and improve their personal scores each time they did the drill.

9.21:   According to cognitive views of motivation we have a need for order and predictability. The behavior of the rod is seemingly counterintuitive, so the students would be motivated to understand why it behaved the way it did.

9.22:   If we base decisions on Maslow's work, we must be sure that students' deficiency needs are met in either case, because if they are not, learners won't progress to the growth needs. High school teachers commonly orient their instruction to the growth needs, tacitly assuming that their students' deficiency needs have been met. This is often an erroneous assumption.

9.23:   Yes, we would assume that a person with a high need for intellectual achievement also has high self-esteem, because—according to Maslow—deficiency needs must be met before learners move to the growth needs.

9.24:   We don't have enough information to make a decision. Because a student prefers working alone doesn't imply that a belonging or self-esteem need is left unmet. The student may prefer working alone for a variety of reasons.

9.25:   Competence motivation relates to both cognitive and social learning views of motivation. A cognitive view would suggest that as people's understanding of the world increases, the need for competence is met until a learner is faced with new tasks needed to cope with the environment. Meeting a need for competence can also lead to feelings of self-efficacy, which is an important concept in social learning views of motivation.

9.26:   Assembly line workers have no control over their work environments. Instead they feel like pawns because their actions are dictated by external factors.

9.27:   A behaviorist might explain achievement motivation by using the concept of reinforcement history. Students high in achievement motivation would have histories of being positively reinforced for achievements, while those low in achievement motivation would have histories of not being consistently reinforced.

9.28:   She would likely select easier dives to perform in competition, and her inclination to avoid challenges would likely result in slower progress than she would make if she had a higher need for achievement.

9.29:   Young children are more egocentric and less likely to think about the skills and achievements of other students. As students become older, this egocentricity decreases, with concomitant increases in social comparisons. In the process of identity formation, students attempt to figure out who they are, defining themselves in terms of their successes and failures. There would be a natural tendency to avoid experiences that would provide painful and potentially negative data for this process.

9.30:   Anne would be easiest to work with because she has a basic idea of the link between achievement and effort. The key to their success is to get them to put in the necessary time and effort. Bob would probably be the hardest to work with because he attributes his failure to lack of ability, which he views as stable and therefore uncontrollable.

9.31:   Effort is unstable and within the learner's control, which means that the possibility exists for different outcomes in the future if effort is increased. In contrast, many people view ability as stable and out of a learner's control, which means that a different outcome in the future is unlikely.

9.32:   Attributing failure to bad luck is preferable to attributing failure to ability. Luck is unstable so the possibility exists for a different outcome in the future.

9.33: Billy's poor grade was attributed to a lack of effort which is internal, unstable and controllable. This attribution allows Billy to believe that he can improve future performance if he increases his effort.

9.34: Bob's comment, "I just can't do this stuff," suggests an entity view of ability, meaning he attributes his poor performance to a stable and uncontrollable lack of ability. To change this view he must experience success on tasks he perceives as worthwhile and then be encouraged to believe that his ability is increasing. (This is difficult, of course, but the long range impact on Bob would be enormous if a teacher could make it happen.)

9.35: One possible explanation is that the student is failure-avoiding, specifically avoiding studying so that the lack of success could be blamed on lack of preparation. If this were the case, he could "fail with honor."

9.36: The best response from the teacher is an acknowledgement that is "on the positive side of neutral." More effusive praise could be viewed as insincere, and the student may also think that you believe he has low ability, which could actually reduce his motivation.

9.37: The most effective way to improve self-efficacy is for the student to experience success on worthwhile tasks. You might work with the student on word problems in math, for example, (because he would almost certainly view them as challenging), offering only enough assistance to assure success. Hopefully, the student's competence will increase, and you can withdraw support until he can successfully complete problems on his own.

9.38: This would be an unwise statement, because it promotes a competitive classroom atmosphere and a performance/ability-focused classroom rather than a learning-focused classroom.

9.39: In this exchange Kathy comments, "It hurts my head, too, when I'm studying and trying to put together some new ideas," followed by "I wish. I have to study every night to keep up with you people." The comments first point out that Kathy studies and that she sometime struggles in the process.

9.40: The effects of enthusiasm are best explained through modeling (part of social learning theory). People tend to imitate behaviors they observe in others, and the likelihood that learners will be enthusiastic about studying a particular topic is increased if they observe a model who is enthusiastic about the topic.

9.41: Using Maslow's work as a basis for the explanation, students in a negative emotional climate don't feel *safe*. Further, being treated sarcastically can detract from *self-esteem*. If safety and/or self-esteem needs are not being met, students are less likely to progress to growth needs, such as intellectual achievement.

9.42: A "two-minute intervention" communicates to students that they're not just another number on the grade ledger or face in the class. By taking the time to personally interact with a student the teacher demonstrates warmth, empathy and caring.

9.43:   Let's look at a brief illustration involving Jeremy, a low achiever, and Sandra, a high achiever.

> T: "What is the first step in solving the problem? Jeremy?"
> J: ". . . I'm not sure."
> T: "Sandra?"
> S: ". . . I'm not sure."
> T: "Look again Sandra. What does the problem ask us for?"

The teacher in this case treated the two students differently. She quickly left Jeremy when he didn't respond, because she didn't expect him to be able to respond. However, when Sandra did the same thing, the teacher prompted her. Over time this differential treatment can strongly affect both motivation and achievement.

9.44:   Social learning views best explain the effects of teacher expectations. Teacher expectations affect the ways teachers treat students. This treatment as we saw in 9.43 impacts students' expectations for their own success, and appropriately high teacher expectations can enhance the value component of the expectancy × value relationship. The combination can increase self-efficacy.

9.45:   The safest question/statement is something such as, "What do you see here," or "Describe what you see for us."

9.46:   Criticism can be a punisher. Using Maslow's work as a basis, criticism reduces the learner's sense of safety (as we saw in 9.41) and criticism damages self-esteem.

9.47:   Success is one of the two factors in expectancy × value theory (expectation for success). Success alone is not sufficient, however. Learners must perceive the task as worthwhile as well (the value component of expectancy × value theory).

9.48:   The statement promotes a ability/performance-focused classroom and an ego orientation rather than a learning-focused classroom with an achievement orientation.

9.49:   An appropriate level of challenge is needed to promote the value component of expectancy × value theory. However, if the challenge becomes so great that the expectation for success disappears, motivation will also disappear.

9.50:   You must do what it takes to help students feel like they can succeed. However, they must also feel that they are succeeding on worthwhile tasks. An effective method is to use some open-ended questions to assure success, then ask higher-level questions to promote challenge and student thinking, and finally provide just enough cues and prompts to assure student success in answering the higher-level questions.

9.51:   As we found in 9.20, timed drills in which students attempt to improve on their past performance can introduce challenge. Team competitions can also be effectively used to promote a sense of challenge.

9.52:   Introductory focus is a form of orienting stimulus.

9.53:   A possible problem might be the following:

> I went to the grocery store and saw a sweater that originally cost $46 marked down 25%. How much would I have to pay for the sweater now?

9.54:   Personalization relates examples to the real world of the students. As both introductory focus and personalization the teacher might ask Reeane and Edward to come to the front of the class and say something such as, "Look everyone. Now, why do you suppose Reeane has blue eyes and Edward has brown ones? What does that tell us about their parents?" If the same students were used as examples in the course of the lesson, they then serve only as a form of personalization.

9.55:   Using an example that is both attractive and personalized, a teacher might start a unit on *Romeo and Juliet* by saying, "Have you ever had friends your parents didn't like? How did it make you feel? What happened? Let's talk about the problem for a minute." Using an attractive example that is not personalized, the teacher might say, "Today we're going to examine a dilemma for two young people. Their families were enemies but they fell in love. We will see how the drama unfolds and how the dilemma affects their lives."

9.56:   *Involvement* and *activity* are closely related but not identical. Activity is a means to aid encoding, and it can occur in a social situation or when someone studies alone. Involvement means learners are "attending and actively participating in the learning activity." Attending and participating includes a social element, with the focus on learner motivation rather than encoding of information.

9.57:   The simplest open-ended question would be one such as, "What do you see here?" A slightly more sophisticated question would be, "How are the picture and the ball alike or different?"

9.58:   Students must be working in an orderly environment in which they feel *safe* before they will be willingly involved.

9.59:   Cognitive views of motivation best explain the need for feedback. According to cognitive theorists, we are motivated by a need for order, predictability, and an understanding of "how the world works." Feedback helps us determine whether or not this understanding is valid.

9.60:   Praise is a positive reinforcer.

9.61:   Open-ended questions have more than one right answer so several different students can answer the same question, all being "correct" without the "correctness" of the answer being at the expense of another student.

9.62:   While Patty put her lesson in the context of the problem with the area of the school grounds, Selinda's exercises on her worksheet were isolated and out of context. Her work sheet would have been more effective if she had embedded the exercises in the context of a written passage.

9.63:   From a cognitive point of view, improvement points indicate that understanding is increasing. From a humanistic view, improvement indicates personal growth which enhances self-esteem. From a behaviorist perspective, improvement is reinforcing and improvement points are reinforcers.

9.64:   The sixth group would consist of Ron, Ann, Charles and Cheryl. The purpose of these groupings is to even out abilities in the groups.

9.65:   Sara would get 20 improvement points. A 98 is 5 points above her base score of 93.

9.66:   Modeling is incorporated when low-ability students observe the learning strategies and attitudes of high-ability students. Success, challenge, and reinforcement are insured by the use of improvement points. Comprehension is accommodated through the incorporation of meaningful learning activities. Involvement occurs as students work together on the teams.

9.67: Cooperative learning strategies work at improving race relations and acceptance of academically handicapped students for two primary reasons. First, students get to know other students as human beings—something that doesn't always happen in traditional, teacher-centered classrooms. Second, students are rewarded for working together, again something that doesn't always happen. Cooperative learning helps build self-esteem by encouraging and even requiring all students to contribute to the team effort. Students who don't typically participate are directly involved in the learning process.

9.68: Another task might include collaborating on the design and conduct of an experiment in science. Two people might perform the actual experiment, a third be the timer and a fourth record data. Gathering information to be included in a matrix would be another example. One student might gather information about the geography of an area, a second about the climate, a third about the economics, and a fourth about the government.

Chapter 10

10.1: A good manager organizes the classroom to promote learning and prevent problems before they occur; a good disciplinarian reacts to student misbehavior and eliminates it. Good managers have students who learn more, because they don't spend as much time and energy in dealing with misbehavior.

10.2: Sondra questioned Judy's authority, when Judy asked her to change seats and she responded, "What did I do?" This type of response is not atypical of junior and senior high students who "test" teachers to see if they are "serious."

10.3: An example of Judy's attempt to develop self-regulated learning occurred when Judy touched Brad on the arm to bring him back to the lesson. This quiet reminder invited Brad to take responsibility for his own learning.

10.4: We would call Judy's actions more authoritative than authoritarian. For example, when Judy disciplined Sondra, she remained calm, reminded Sondra of the rule, and evenly explained how her behaviors were affecting Judy's teaching.

10.5: While the answers to this question will vary, some aspects of management that typically contribute to learning include maximizing time devoted to instruction, the lesson staying focused and uninterrupted, and students cooperating and answering questions. Management problems that detract from learning include disorganized lessons, unruly students talking and interrupting the lesson, lack of attention, and lack of student participation.

10.6: According to cognitive theories, we are motivated by a need for order and predictability and well-managed classrooms are orderly. Also, learning can be a motivating activity in and of itself, because it leads to feelings of self-efficacy—according to social learning views of motivation. Well-managed classrooms allow learning to take place.

10.7: In both cases Judy implemented a *responsibility model* by responding quickly and firmly in an attempt to apply logical consequences and help the students learn from their actions.

10.8: According to Piaget, younger children are more egocentric and are more perceptual and concrete than are their older counterparts. This is reflected in their need for rules that are explicitly taught and practiced. According to Erikson, students are motivated by an increasing desire to be independent, which is most manifested in adolescence during the crisis of identity vs. confusion. This is reflected in the need for a firm foundation of stability, explicit boundaries and predictable outcomes.

10.9: You could check by simply placing it on the overhead and walking to rear of the class to check it yourself. If you've forgotten to do this, put the transparency up and ask a student at the back of the class to read it.

10.10: Under these conditions, the best arrangement would probably be to face the students toward the right wall and away from the window. They could still see the screen on the front wall by merely turning their heads to their left.

10.11: Warm-up activities involve students in academic tasks while the teacher takes roll and completes other beginning-of-class routines, and they also bridge the gap between previous lessons and the one to come. Warm-up activities might include the following: a) math—have the students solve a problem or two similar to their homework for the day; b) science—write a question on the board that requires students to summarize information from the previous day; c) English—have the students produce some examples of a concept—such as indirect objects—or a grammar rule that they studied the previous day.

10.12: The answer to this question will vary, but most procedures in college classrooms are less explicit than they are at the public school level, because there is less need for explicit procedures with college students. However, your instructor may have made some comments about procedures, such as starting times and how tests and papers will be returned.

10.13: The thrust of the rule is twofold—listen when someone else has the floor, and when you have the floor you have the right to be listened to. Judy handled Sondra's infraction of the rule by helping her understand how her actions were interfering with the process of teaching and learning.

10.14: "Instantly knowing" best illustrates the concept of *automaticity* from our study of information processing.

10.15: Cooperatively discussing rules results in student input and ownership, which illustrates internal control.

10.16: We have been essentially consistent with our own guidelines. For instance, the guidelines are stated clearly and positively, and the list is short. Rationales for the guidelines are provided in the text of the chapter. While not explicit, we have gotten student input from the first edition of the text which is reflected in this edition.

10.17: A first grade teacher might need to make the rules less abstract and more behavioral (e.g., "Remain completely quiet if a classmate answers a question incorrectly," instead of "Treat the teacher and your classmates with respect."). An eleventh grade teacher might want to add, "Do your own work," and talk about the importance of honesty and homework. This basic list works surprisingly well for most grade levels, however.

10.18: Effective concept teaching involves the use of positive and negative examples to teach abstract ideas. Martha effectively modeled desired behaviors (positive examples); if she had anticipated any common mistakes she might have modeled and discussed these as negative examples.

10.19: As he taught the rule for bringing materials to class, Jordi first asked the students to explain the rationale for the rules, and what could happen if they didn't bring their materials. In the process he helped them understand the link between the rule and outcomes, which captures elements of problem solving. Short term, this increases the likelihood that the rules will be followed; long term, it teaches students to think about their behavior and the consequences of their actions.

10.20: This is the point where it would be a good idea to praise the students for following the rules and procedures as well as they have, reminding the students about them again, and asking them to explain carefully and specifically why the rules and procedures are important.

10.21: During this stage students are wrestling with the crisis of industry/inferiority. If the student is generally unsuccessful in academic tasks, the disruptive behavior may be a misdirected attempt to compensate, or be "successful at disruption," to help meet this need. While admittedly difficult, the first step would be to try and help the student be more successful academically.

10.22: When Sondra did not want to move, Judy patiently but firmly reminded her of the rule and required her to comply.

10.23: Glasser's and Dreikurs' work do not emphasize immediate consequences—such as reinforcers and punishers—for student behavior. Instead they focus on cognitive approaches which focus on helping students understand the importance of rules and which emphasize self versus external control. For these reasons they would not be called behavioral.

10.24: With third graders, you could explain the rule, then explicitly model it yourself in a role play situation, which would be followed by pointing out examples in a learning activity. Typically, seventh graders have been exposed to this rule, so it merely needs to be clearly described. (Identifying examples of students raising their hands to speak during a learning activity is also a good idea with seventh graders.)

10.25: Procedures that describe what students should be doing during the beginning of class and during transition times are effective for filling "dead time." Judy Holmquist's procedure of having a problem on the overhead when students came in the room is a good example.

10.26: Judy demonstrated withitness when she heard Alison mutter and knew Kevin had poked Alison. She then moved near Kevin and asked him the next question. She intervened immediately and "caught the right one."

10.27: The teacher's behavior illustrates *overlapping*. The teacher could apply variable interval reinforcement by periodically (and unpredictably) getting up from her reading group and moving among the students doing seatwork and praising them for being on task as she went. She could make the process more formal by awarding tokens to those on task, which could be exchanged for rewards at the end of the day or week.

10.28: This teacher's intervening comment leaves the discussion of cells dangling. If she returns to the discussion of cells she has "flip-flopped" in her presentation. Both are obstacles to smoothness. We don't have enough evidence about her maintenance of momentum to make a conclusion.

10.29: The third grader noticed that the teacher's eyes got bigger, that she looked right at the student, didn't move, changed the tone of her voice, and that sometimes she "stands over us and looks down at us." The student noticed proximity, eye contact, body orientation, and vocal variation.

10.30: Caring can be communicated through eye contact, body orientation (orienting directly toward the receiver), and proximity (moving closer). As we saw in chapter 9, the best indicator of caring is the willingness to spend time with the student. Firmness is indicated with loudness and tone of voice in addition to eye contact, proximity, and direct body orientation.

10.31: An alternate teacher response might include, "I cannot teach when people are whispering, and I get frustrated when I can't teach, because this is important." This message: 1) identifies the behavior (whispering), 2) describes its effect on the teacher (can't teach); and 3) describes how it makes the teacher feel (frustrated).

10.32: Based on the available information, student talking and students coming late to class are teacher problems because they can interrupt the class. Homework not completed would be a student problem. Helpful additional information would be knowing whether or not the talking and coming late is disruptive or whether it affects only the individual students.

10.33: An assertive response including an "I-message" could be, "John, I can't be heard when someone sharpens a pencil while I'm teaching, and I get upset when I can't be heard. Sit down and use this pencil." (Then give the student a short pencil from a box, to use until the learning activity is over.)

10.34: The teacher didn't demonstrate the characteristics of active listening. In returning to her work she didn't devote her full attention to the student, nor did she respond to the intellectual and emotional content of the student's message.

10.35: Increased parental involvement also helps parents become better informed about school activities and their importance. This information puts them in a better position to help their youngsters with academic tasks and also increases the likelihood that they will offer more encouragement, which can increase student motivation.

10.36: The present school is a stimulus similar to a conditioned stimulus (the parents' own school experiences), so the present school elicits conditioned responses similar to the original conditioned responses (the angers, disappointments, and nervous stomachs Rich identifies in the quote). The parents generalize—emotionally—from their own experiences to the present school.

10.37: Three simple techniques would be to write letters to the parents in their native languages, learn to verbally greet parents in their native languages, and invite students to attend conferences with their parents to help translate information for the parents.

10.38: A basic comprehension-checking strategy is asking questions. This might be done over the phone with the parents, in a face-to-face conference or by sharing the letters with another teacher.

10.39: The letter demonstrates firmness by taking a proactive approach to classroom management, clearly communicating expectations. Caring is communicated through the tone of the letter which is positive and upbeat. Because the letter elicits the cooperation of both students and parents it is also democratic.

10.40: Perhaps the most effective way of communicating caring is calling parents on teachers' personal time, such as in the evening. Even if the call is unproductive, it communicates that teachers care enough to spend their personal time to help students. Teachers can also send notes, letters, and work samples home, and greet students and parents together when parents bring their children to school.

10.41: Cindy is applying the concepts of *cuing, modeling, positive reinforcement,* and *vicarious conditioning.* Her comment is a cue for the rest of the class, she is attempting to use Ted as a model for the rest of the students, Ted is being positively reinforced, and the rest of the class is being vicariously reinforced.

10.42: One example would be assigning extra homework problems in a math class as punishers for misbehavior. Similarly, assigning an essay in English for misbehavior would be using classwork as a punisher.

10.43: There are least two possible explanations for teachers' tendency to focus on undesirable behaviors. First, because of the complexity of classroom activities, desirable behavior tends to "melt" into the overall flow of teaching and learning, while misbehavior is simply more noticeable. Second, in most classrooms desirable behaviors considerably outnumber undesirable ones, making it impossible to focus on all them. Focusing on a few then requires careful judgment—to avoid a perception of favoritism—which further increases classroom complexity.

10.44: All of the rewards except food are secondary reinforcers. Younger children need to be helped to see the link between secondary reinforcers and good behavior, while older students have already made this connection.

10.45: Assertive Discipline is considered behavioral because it focuses on the consequences of behavior—reinforcers for desirable behavior and punishers for undesirable behavior.

10.46: Overly long management interventions interfere with lesson *momentum,* and specifically *overdwelling.*

10.47: Judy remained with Sondra until Sondra moved. She stayed and watched to be certain of compliance before she turned her full attention away from Sondra.

10.48: Consistency strongly relates to Piaget's concept of *equilibrium.* Consistently enforced rules allow students to predict the consequences of their behaviors, making the environment understandable, which allows students to remain at equilibrium.

10.49: A possible I-message might be the following: "Student talking interrupts my teaching, this makes me lose my train of thought and I get annoyed when my train of thought is disrupted."

10.50: The attention of other students is a common reinforcer. Also, misbehavior can allow the student to avoid academic tasks, which can be negatively reinforcing if the student is unable to succeed on the tasks. The reinforcers must be eliminated if ignoring undesirable behavior is going to work.

10.51: Young children are much more responsive to teachers' praise than are older ones. They still view teachers as surrogate parents and the influence of peers is not as strong.

10.52: Many behaviors are learned through modeling. Rough desists are modeled behaviors which students can then imitate. Rough desists increasing behavior can also be explained from a cognitive point of view. Learners form a schemata for the environment, and this schemata describes disruptive behavior as acceptable.

10.53: Logical consequences is a cognitive strategy that places students in a problem solving mode and encourages them to find connections between their behaviors and subsequent results. Because of these characteristics, logical consequences is a central component of the Responsibility Model.

10.54: Since ignoring Jason's behavior hasn't produced positive results in the past, ignoring the behavior would now communicate lack of commitment to her policy. At this point she needs to apply a consequence. Later, if his behavior improves, and he *briefly* talks to one of his buddies, she may choose to ignore the behavior.

10.55: Glasser's approach teaches responsibility by encouraging students to form links between their actions and the consequences of those actions. For instance, the teacher in the episode helped Michael see that running to get in line resulted in Susan being pushed. The teacher in the episode encouraged problem solving by asking Michael to suggest what should be done.

10.56: Making an effort to have the student feel accepted addresses the caring dimension. Firmness and follow-through are illustrated in the adherence to the ten steps. Consistency comes through a clear focus on the unacceptable behaviors. Power struggles are minimized by the teacher working individually with students out of the classroom.

10.57: In dealing with violence and aggression immediate actions are called for. Short-term actions would be at "applying consequences" end of the continuum. Other interventions are skipped because of the seriousness of the act and the need to immediately stop the problem.

10.58: Research indicates that problem solving simulations can be helpful. In using simulations you might ask the student to recreate the circumstances leading up to the earlier fights. Another strategy is to involve parents and school personnel such as the guidance counselor or school psychologist.

Chapter 11

11.1: Beginners need to write much more detailed plans because their teaching schemata are less developed and fewer of their teaching skills are automatic. As an intern, you would probably write plans that are more detailed than Ron's, but they may not be as involved as Mai's unless they are required by your supervisor.

11.2: Planning is involved in the preparation of procedures and rules. Planning influences organization which affects lesson momentum and smoothness, which also affect management.

11.3: A teacher anticipating a less motivated class might plan for an introductory activity that attracts attention and pulls them into the lesson. Some simple examples would be blowing between two pieces of paper and seeing that they come together rather than blow apart, having a student run across the front of the room and describing her actions to illustrate parts of speech, or coming into the classroom dressed as a gold miner to begin a unit on westward expansion in history.

11.4: Research indicates that teachers who are carefully following a plan typically continue to follow the plan whether or not the lesson is succeeding. The plan is a form of security, and abandoning it would disrupt the teacher's equilibrium.

11.5: His procedures are in his head and are the products of years of experience, learning what works and what doesn't.

11.6: While both the teachers evidenced reflection, Ron was probably the more reflective of the two. As a beginning teacher Mai was concerned about her teaching and was constantly trying to figure out what works. Her professional growth depends on reflection. Because of his experience, Ron's teaching and management procedures were more automatic, affording him more time and energy to be reflective.

11.7: The lack of a specifically stated goal does not imply that Ron was not following the Linear Rational Model. In fact, we can infer that Ron had a very clear goal in mind (for the students to understand kinetic theory), and the selection and organization of his learning activity was closely aligned with his goal (his bottles, balloons, and model). However, we have no evidence about his evaluation procedures, and in this regard he departed from the model.

11.8: An objective written according to Mager's format might be, "Given a passage students haven't read, they will identify the main idea in each paragraph." *Given the passage* is the condition, *identify* is the behavior, and *each* is the criterion.

11.9: Using Gronlund's format the object might appear as follows:

Understands main idea
1. Describes main idea
2. Identifies main idea in a paragraph
3. Correctly uses main idea in a paragraph

11.10: While Mai's objectives don't follow either format exactly, they more closely follow Gronlund's. They identify a general goal and specific behaviors that will be used as evidence that the goal has been reached, which are consistent with Gronlund's format.

11.11: Conceptually, lack of instructional alignment cannot be the fault of the objective. If the assessment and learning activity are congruent, but not consistent with the objective, they are simply aimed at another objective. For example, if the goal is for students to be able to write paragraphs using descriptive adjectives, but the learning activity has the students recognize adjectives in sentences and the assessment also has them recognize adjectives in sentences, neither the learning activity nor the assessment are directed at the objective.

11.12: Ron's sequence was an inductive one which began with an attention-getting activity. An alternate sequence would be to begin with a short introduction to kinetic theory. This latter sequence has the advantage of being highly structured but it has the disadvantage of probably being less motivating than the one Ron chose.

11.13: A brief task analysis might appear as follows:

Terminal Behavior: Using adverbs in sentences
Prerequisite Skills: 1) Define *adverb*
2) Locate adverbs in sentences
3) Identify instances when these are used correctly and incorrectly (e.g., "He played good." vs. "He played well.")
4) Use adverbs correctly in sentences.
Sequence: The objectives listed above should be in proper sequence.
Diagnose: Develop an instrument that has four sections corresponding to the above skills.

11.14: Because subtraction with regrouping is more hierarchical—it has a series of prerequisite skills that are needed to master it—than understanding the animal classes, a task analysis for subtraction is more valuable than one for the animal classes.

11.15: A logical analysis of objectives, learning activities, and assessment instruments, as found in the Linear Rational Model, is equally important when using a constructivist frame of reference. Teachers still need to consider their goals, and design learning and assessment activities that are congruent with those goals.

11.16: Mai Ling's lesson plan specifically stated that her lesson was embedded in a larger unit on decimals. Since it wasn't specified, we would have to infer that Ron's lesson was embedded in a larger unit on the behavior of gases.

11.17: The Jacobsen et al. format is more closely aligned with the Linear Rational Model because it clearly specifies how the objective will be evaluated—a critical component in this model. The Moore model attends more to instructional procedures, closure and assignments. It may also be more helpful in planning for motivation, because it has a specific provision for an introduction, and introductory focus is a component of the Model for Promoting Student Motivation, which we studied in chapter 9.

11.18: The lower primary grades place more emphasis on affective and psychomotor goals while the upper grades tend to focus more on cognitive goals. This narrowing focus can ignore students' needs, particularly in the affective domain, that have an important influence on learning, and therefore, the trend is unfortunate.

11.19: Mai Ling's first objective is at the comprehension level. Her second is difficult to classify without knowing the context in which the conversions will take place. If the students are given word problems in which converting fractions to decimals is part of the decision they make in solving the problem, the objective is at the application level. If it merely involves following a pattern, as in using an algorithm, it is at the comprehension level.

11.20: While Kelly Ryan's objective appears to be at the application level, it merely involves the application of an algorithm, so it is at the comprehension level.

11.21: Both were interested in having students respond at least at the valuing level—Ron in science and Mai in math. Evidence for this is Ron's comment, "One of the things I'm after is for them to get over their fear of science. Otherwise they'll take only what's required in high school." This might suggest that Ron is aiming at the Organization level where they would act upon their values by taking more science in high school. Mai agreed with Ron's general goal, saying "Math is sort of the same way, although they start out scared and then they get so they don't like it."

11.22: Weight training involves the development of endurance, strength and flexibility and would be targeted at *physical abilities*.

11.23: Some advantages of centralized curricula are that they ensure that all students in the state or district have access to the same knowledge, and minimum standards are met. Arguments against centralized curricula include the decline of individual teacher autonomy. There isn't a clear answer to the question, and it remains a controversial issue.

11.24: When students are given objectives their effort focuses on content related to the objectives and they tend to spend less time and energy on other information.

11.25: There are several rationales for this. One is that the *process* helps preservice teachers learn to think systematically about their teaching. Second, lesson plans are like "think-alouds" that have been studied in the cognitive strategy research. They make the novice teacher's thoughts visible for reflection and for analysis and evaluation by other students and the instructor. Finally, detailed, written plans are useful when candidates first teach.

11.26: It is unlikely that requiring detailed plans would improve teaching. It might make teachers more thoughtful and reflective if the process was approached with a positive attitude, but veteran teachers' use past experience as an important factor in their planning, and given the varied demands on teachers, requiring detailed plans would probably pull energies away from other aspects of teaching. Further, veterans would probably resist the process, and requiring the plans could result in resentment in the teachers.

11.27: Veteran teachers changing assignments (e.g., a first grade teacher switched to fourth grade or a biology teacher switched to chemistry) report that their planning activities are more detailed. They still bring with them existing schemata about how to plan, manage and teach, but they initially need to be more detailed in their planning because of the change.

11.28: In addition to providing extra time, teachers can help slower students by providing extra instructional support. This might be in the form of additional teacher help, peer tutoring, extra practice and feedback, or additional learning materials.

11.29: In addition to extra time, mastery learning also provides corrective instruction based on students' performance on formative quizzes. For example, if a student misses items related to addition with regrouping, the teacher would provide corrective instruction specifically targeting this problem. The advantage is the fact that students get additional instruction and practice; this disadvantage is the additional work and record keeping that is required from the instructor.

11.30: There are many content areas where information and skills are basic and cumulative, such as math. In these areas student choices are necessarily limited. However, even in basic skill areas like reading, students can practice the skills using books of their choice. As students get older, they are usually able to make more considered choices, so allowing student choice when possible is advisable. Helping students learn to make wise and thoughtful choices is a worthwhile goal at any level.

11.31: The advantages of locating computers in classrooms are that they are readily accessible to students, so integrating them into the regular curriculum is easier. However, providing enough computers so that all students have access to them involves huge costs, and many teachers are still not well enough trained to fully exploit computers' capabilities. Labs have the advantage of more reasonable cost and access to trained teachers; their disadvantages are accessibility and not being integrated into the regular curriculum.

11.32: Tutorials are similar to drill and practice software in that they provide practice with feedback. They are different in that subsequent instruction with tutorials is varied and matched to students' responses. When drill and practice programs are used, they should be monitored closely by the teacher to ensure that instruction is matched to student needs.

11.33: Cost (assuming the computers already exist), time and the ability to analyze experimental results that can't be obtained any other way are advantages. A disadvantage is that students may develop an inaccurate view of science based on the tidy, precise results these electronic experiments provide. Science isn't neat, clean, and linear; it's often messy and frustrating.

11.34: Thinking about thinking relates to the topic of *metacognition.* One of our major goals as teachers should be to help students become aware of their thinking processes and how these effect learning.

Chapter 12

12.1: Shirley's students were learning the concept *equivalent fractions,* and she taught them the algorithm for finding equivalent fractions. An algorithm is a type of academic rule.

12.2: In chapter 8, we discussed the different kinds of cognitive learning outcomes, and pointed out that different forms of learning required different types of instruction. Robert Gagne was the person most responsible for originally promoting the idea.

12.3:   Constructivism strongly relates to Piaget's work. The suggestion that learners actively construct their own understanding, which requires teachers to guide students rather than merely deliver content to passive learners has been a major influence on our present views of thinking.

12.4:   The allocated time would be the class time as stated in the schedule of classes. While instructors have no control over the allocated time for classes, they are in total control over the amount of time they allocate to specific topics.

12.5:   To answer this question note when the instructor typically begins actual teaching and when he or she stops instruction. Also, note the time spent in noninstructional activities, such as explaining class procedures and collecting and passing back papers, which are the kinds of activities that compete with instructional time.

12.6:   Teacher talk is only one kind of instruction. Time spent on student responses and reports, group projects, small group discussions, and seatwork is all instructional time if it focuses on course content.

12.7:   The shaded portion is the time students are not involved in a learning activity or are not paying attention. Teachers can narrow this segment by making lessons highly interactive, involving students in groupwork and varying their learning activities.

12.8:   Probably the most widely used indicator of on-task behavior is eye contact. Other indicators include raising hands, responding in class, question asking, body orientation—upright and leaning towards the teacher. (Working on problems or exercises during seatwork is, of course, one of the most accurate indicators.)

12.9:   Self-efficacy includes a *value* component, or the extent to which the learning activity is worthwhile and challenging. Academic learning time focuses only on a student's success in the learning activity. (Both self-efficacy and academic learning time assume that the learner is engaged.) The concept of *self-efficacy* implies that we must try to design challenging learning activities that students perceive as valuable, not merely provide success on trivial tasks.

12.10:   As we saw in our study of Erikson's work, the elementary grades are the time when feelings of industry vs. inferiority develop. Successfully meeting classroom challenges results in the development of industry.

12.11:   If students answer incorrectly in question-and-answer sessions, the teacher can intervene immediately. If students are unsuccessful on a homework assignment, usually no one is there to provide assistance.

12.12:   Experienced teachers have well established classroom routines, and they are skilled at monitoring the students' behaviors while conducting interactive instruction, such as questioning students. They quickly notice when a learning activity isn't working, and they adapt their instruction. Beginners' routines are less well established, they are more "mechanical" in their instruction, and they are less able to adapt when the activity isn't working. Experienced teachers acquire these skills with conscious effort and practice.

12.13:   If you're typical, some attitudes you probably will cite are: open to other points of view, willing to help, fair, and enthusiastic about what they're teaching.

12.14:   While the only level of time not influenced by organization is allocated time, instructional time is most directly affected by organization. Engaged and academic learning time are indirectly affected.

12.15: Introducing her lesson with this problem was a form of introductory focus, which corresponds to an orienting stimulus in the information processing model. (The "cakes" also provided context for the rest of the lesson and ultimately aided encoding by making the content more meaningful for the students.)

12.16: Her sequence allowed her to capitalize on the process of elaboration. The students elaborated on their understanding of adding fractions with like denominators to develop an understanding of adding fractions with unlike denominators. (Shirley's teaching also put the students in an active role, which is another factor that aids encoding.)

12.17: Thorough planning is the best way to ensure language clarity. This includes study so teachers have a clear understanding of the content they're teaching, followed by careful organization so that ideas can be presented clearly. Developing the ability to monitor your own language as you teach can help during lessons. Videotaping your teaching can give you valuable feedback about your language.

12.18: Scrambled discourse makes it difficult for learners to *organize* the ideas they're studying. Scrambled discourse can indirectly detract from elaboration as well, because the link between old and new information is not clear.

12.19: Smooth transitions result from effective organization, which allow the shift from one activity to another with minimal loss of time. A transition *signal* is a form of verbal communication that tells learners a shift from one topic to another is taking place. A clear transition signal can help make a transition smoother.

12.20: Emphasis highlights important information and is a form of orienting stimulus. Because it increases attention, it indirectly aids encoding.

12.21: By introducing the lesson with her problem and concrete objects, Shirley provided a context in which the remainder of the lesson was placed. The context and concrete objects increased the lesson's meaningfulness, which aided encoding. Because the information was meaningfully encoded, it was easier to retrieve.

12.22: Most commonly, the examples used to illustrate the content provides the sensory focus.

12.23: Sensory focus is critical for young learners because attention and meta-attention are less well developed in young than they are in older learners. Introductory focus increases in importance for older learners who are more apt to question the importance of the content they're learning. In addition, because topics taught to older learners are often complex and abstract, academic focus is important to help make the content meaningful.

12.24: Feedback is more important after an incorrect answer. A correct answer indicates that the student knows the answer and no adjustment in schemata is required. Without feedback for an incorrect answer, learners may retain a misconception or even develop a new one. This is consistent with an information processing view. A behaviorist, however, would have the opposite reaction. For behaviorists, learning takes place when desired behaviors are reinforced. To capitalize on reinforcement, learners must supply the desired behaviors. While behaviorists provide feedback for incorrect answers as well, there is no mechanism in behaviorism for promoting learning until the learner displays the desired behavior.

12.25: Karen gave a correct but uncertain response, while Jon gave a correct and confident answer. Shirley was alert enough to recognize the difference and responded specifically to Karen's answer while merely replying "Excellent" to Jon.

12.26: As we lecture, we primarily monitor students' nonverbal behaviors for signs of inattention or lack of understanding; when questioning, we monitor their responses both for accuracy and the confidence with which they respond; in discussions we monitor students' participation to be certain as many as possible are involved and to be sure the discussion remains focused on the theme; and during seatwork we monitor the students to be sure they are working and are being successful. Lecture is the most difficult to monitor, because all we can do is make inferences on the basis of the students' nonverbal behaviors. This is another reason lecture is the least effective teaching method.

12.27: Repetition and review are similar but not identical. Repetition is the simple reiteration of a specific point. Review summarizes prior learning and is used as a basis for elaboration or as a form of closure at the end of a lesson.

12.28: For young or low ability students and with difficult content you would review more frequently and more specifically. You would also provide additional concrete examples during the review.

12.29: While the answer to this question is individual, most commonly teachers ask questions and allow anyone who desires to do so to call out an answer. When students are unable to respond correctly, the question is turned to another student. More effective questions are directed to individuals by name, and when they are unable to answer, they are prompted.

12.30: In addition to being called on equally, all students should be given similar amounts of time to answer, prompted when they are unable to answer, and given feedback with corrective information. Students should be also be given similar support affectively and nonverbally, such as leaning toward them, facing them directly and smiling at them.

12.31: Questions remaining focused on academic content most closely relates to *academic focus,* which simply means staying on the subject. They also indirectly relate to *connected discourse* which means the lesson is thematic and leads to a point.

12.32: A teacher who says "Can someone help out?" is negatively reinforcing the student for not responding. The student sits quietly or says "I don't know," and the teacher then removes the question, which increases the likelihood of the student not responding the next time he or she is "on the spot."

12.33: Simply, wait-time gives both teachers and students time to think. For teachers it provides them with time to think about the direction of the lesson and student responses. For students it reduces pressure to answer quickly and encourages more students to think about the question.

12.34: This form of interaction dominates for at least two reasons. First, it helps maintain classroom control, one of the primary concerns for teachers. Also, the process is relatively simple for teachers, so their own working memories are not overloaded with simultaneously trying to lead student discussions, encourage involvement and keep order. The problem with this pattern is that the classroom environment is often competitive, so lower achievers are left out, and student responses are based on teacher reinforcement rather then their own ideas.

12.35: If low achievers are admonished for calling out when they know an answer—since they don't have established patterns of success—their inclination to try and participate can be reduced. Similarly, students who come from home environments that tolerate (or even promote) interruptions can experience cultural conflict if they are admonished for interrupting, and they may also become less inclined to participate.

12.36: Active involvement, open-ended questions, and appropriate wait-times are effective for all students. For confident students who are already inclined to participate, the number of open-ended questioning would probably be reduced, but asking open-ended questions is still worthwhile.

12.37: Understanding equivalent fractions is not a procedural skill. Being able to form an equivalent fraction for 2/3, for example, *is* a procedural skill.

12.38: Rules and procedural skills are closely related but not synonymous. A rule is declarative knowledge, and a procedural skill is the procedural knowledge application of the rule. For example, knowing the rule for subject-verb agreement is a form of declarative knowledge. Being able to write using subject-verb agreement correctly is a procedural skill.

12.39: *Teacher centrality* is a term similar to *active teaching*. They both mean that the teacher is the one delivering the content to the students—either with an expository or a guided discovery format—rather than having students get the information from reading or worksheets. *Task orientation* means that instructional and engaged time are maximized to their fullest and the focus is on learning rather than socialization or some other nonacademic activity, and *high structure* means that the classroom environment is orderly and predictable, routines are in place, and rules are followed.

12.40: Effective teaching is the entire set of teacher behaviors that have been found to increase student achievement. Direct instruction is the subset of effective teaching that focuses on teaching procedural skills. Direct instruction is based primarily on a behavioral view of learning. Students are presented skills, which they practice, and which they are reinforced for correctly demonstrating. While direct instruction doesn't prohibit embedding the skills in context and using a constructivist approach to teaching, the skills are typically presented by the teacher out of context.

12.41: Shirley's introductory focus—her concrete and visual cardboard "cakes" together with the problem of adding a third of one to half of the other, which provided context for the lesson—helped draw the students into the lesson. Her energy and enthusiastic manner also helped motivate the students.

12.42: If success rates are high, meaning the students are answering most of the questions correctly, and they are asking questions of their own, the teacher can move to guided practice. Until then, the teacher should continue with the whole-group activity until students appear to be ready to work independently.

12.43: The first three students having trouble indicates that the class doesn't "get it." He should quickly check a couple more students to confirm that the class is having trouble, and if they are, he should stop the seatwork and reteach the lesson. (Trying to respond to all the students' questions individually is inefficient, is likely to lead to reduced effort, and can lead to management problems.)

12.44: Teacher talk is often high during the *introduction and review* and *presentation* phases, sharply reduced during the *guided practice* phase, and minimal during the *independent practice* phase. Teacher talk goes down as the lesson progresses, because more of the responsibility is being placed on the students.

12.45: Assignments, since they're predictable and based on time, follow a fixed-interval schedule, the disadvantage of which is reduced effort immediately after reinforcers are given and minimal effort until just before the next reinforcer is given. Shortening the interval (giving frequent assignments) increases the frequency of efforts.

12.46: Shirley's problem of adding a third and a half a cake was her *anticipatory set*. She then asked "How am I going to figure it out?" and continued, "That's what we're going to learn about today." This statement provided her *objective and purpose*. *Input* was provided when she demonstrated that 1/3 and 2/6 and 1/4 and 3/12 were equivalent, *modeling* an algorithm for finding equivalent fractions during the demonstrations. She constantly *checked for understanding* during the process. *Guided* and *independent practice* came at the end of the lesson.

12.47: The teacher might have the students make four groups of 10 interlocking cubes and five loose cubes beside the groups. She could then have them hold up one of the groups of 10 and describe it, being sure that they said something such as, "This is one group of 10 cubes." She could then have them describe how many groups of 10 they had and how many loose ones they had. She could then write the numeral 45 on the chalkboard and have the students describe the four, carefully linking it (verbally) to the four groups of 10, and verbally linking the 5 to the five loose cubes. (A problem with the lesson as described is that merely circling the tally marks isn't concrete enough for the students to conceptualize that they are supposed to represent a group.)

12.48: Shirley's problem was finding out how much cake she had if she added a third of one to half of the other.

12.49: The concept from chapter 2 is *intellectual empathy*.

12.50: You could ask the students if the position of the cup in the water would matter, since the cup is keeping the air out. They should conclude no, because if the position mattered, something other than the cup must be involved. You could tip the cup sideways (letting the trapped air out), and the cup would fill with water. You could also put the cup in the bowl right side up, and they would again see that the cup filled with water.

12.51: Shirley did a better job than did Keisha. Shirley began her lesson with her cardboard "cakes" and the practical problem of taking a third of one and half of the other. The lesson then focused on finding a solution to the problem. While Keisha's students were involved in a worthwhile discussion, no practical application was involved in the lesson.

12.52: Organized bodies of knowledge are usually compilations of declarative knowledge. They involve being able to state relationships among different forms of content. They include facts, concepts, generalizations, principles, and perhaps even rules, but they don't focus on any of these specific forms of content.

12.53: Commonly, effective lecturers demonstrate some combination of the following characteristics: They are dynamic and enthusiastic, and they use clear language to present their information in a well organized sequence utilizing many examples. They review and reiterate important points, spend minimal time on extraneous information, and the lecture has a primary thread which leads to a point. Each of these behaviors will transfer to elementary and secondary classrooms.

12.54: Working memory has limited capacity and is a bottleneck for incoming information. If too much information is presented without allowing students time to process it, it will be lost instead of encoded into long-term memory. Teachers can use repetition and frequent reviews to help overcome the limitations of working memory.

12.55: Comprehension-monitoring capitalizes on both activity and elaboration. Students are put in an active role when teachers ask them to describe their understanding of the lecture portion of the lesson, and their descriptions will be an expansion of their present understanding, which is a form of elaboration.

12.56: Two concepts from behaviorism can be used to answer the question. First, questions are forms of cues that induce responses, which can then be reinforced. Second, question and answer activities use a variable-ratio reinforcement schedule, which promotes behaviors that are more enduring than any other schedule.

12.57: Carrie's presented the problem of trying to explain why the Mexican child looked so different from either the Spanish or Brazilian child.

12.58: Typically, problems used for discussion involve issues or questions that don't have cut-and-dried answers. Open-ended problems, such as the one in chapter 8 involving voter apathy, could be used for discussions. Discussions of different approaches to a solution for the lemonade problem are also appropriate. This is the type of thing Keisha Coleman did with her students.

12.59: If the students are unable (or unwilling) to read the text and comprehend the information, she might prepare (either alone or with the students' help) a chart in which the information is summarized. The students' backgrounds could then be developed through a discussion of the information on the chart.

12.60: The skills must be specifically taught. The most effective method is to use a simulation, where the teacher directly and specifically models the skills. Short written case studies, in which the skills are illustrated, can also be effective.

12.61: The discussion should be stopped and another learning activity should be substituted in which the background needed to conduct the discussion would be developed. To continue the discussion without adequate background disintegrates into a "bull session" and is a waste of time.

12.62: David only required his students to identify similarities and differences based on information directly in front of the students. This process was open-ended, meaning that a variety of responses would be acceptable. Mary's students were solving problems which required a single correct answer, and the solutions had to come from the students' backgrounds. This was much more demanding than the task David gave his students.

12.63: Stacey's students had to make observations about magnets and magnetic materials, David's had to compare the Jamestown and Plymouth Colonies, and Mary's had to solve problems involving areas of geometric shapes.

12.64: Stacey's and David's students were making observations and comparisons respectively, which were open-ended activities. Mary's students were getting solutions to specific problems, so it was easy for her to monitor the students' progress, making a specified amount of time less important.

12.65: Stacey's students had to produce a paper on which observations were written, David's a paper which contained the comparisons, and Mary's a paper with the solutions to the problems.

12.66: David's would be more effective. Since his students only had to identify similarities and differences, and the information was in front of the students, low achievers could more easily contribute to the group than they could in Mary's activity where specific solutions based on the students' backgrounds were required. In her case the lower achievers in the group would likely defer to the higher achievers, and the positive effects of the groupwork would be diminished.

Chapter 13

13.1: The answer to this question will vary. Some likely elements are tests, quizzes, and some project work, such as written assignments, research papers, and the written products of cooperative learning activities.

13.2: Both daily and weekly quizzes use a fixed-interval reinforcement schedule, which produces "scallops" where behaviors increase just before reinforcement and decrease right after reinforcement. Daily quizzes produce smaller "scallops" (students study every day rather than only on Thursday—assuming the quiz is given Friday).

13.3: Teachers should describe in general terms what the test will cover, the format for testing, and the kinds of responses that will be expected. However, if the exact content is specified, students limit their study to that content, and overall learning is reduced. Frequently missed items should be discussed in class, and students should have the opportunity to discuss all the items they missed in private if they choose to do so. Not all test items can be discussed in class because the process is time consuming, and it is not a good use of time for students who answer most of the items correctly.

13.4: While answers to this question will vary, testing can detract from motivation if it is infrequent (e.g., a mid-term and final), if the tests don't match what has been taught, if scoring seems arbitrary and if feedback is delayed or vague.

13.5: Informal measurement included Kathy's checking students' seatwork as she circulated around the class and her giving two problems every day at the beginning of class.

13.6: An example of a systematic assessment would be a test or quiz, for which the teacher planned and prepared the students. Unsystematic assessments would be responses from students in question and answer sessions or observations of students' nonverbal behaviors.

13.7: *Congruent* can be illustrated with two circles labeled "measurement" and "goals." If these two circles overlap completely, then the measurement is congruent with the goals. The terms *congruent* and *consistent* are not synonymous. Measurements can be consistent but not fit stated goals, so they would not be congruent.

13.8: An example would be a measurement written in English for a student whose English is limited. Another example would be a test item that assumes common cultural background, which the student may not have.

13.9: Based only on the information we have in the directions, the first grade has questionable validity, since the teacher didn't specify that one of their grades depended on creativity. The grade for punctuation is valid if it is reliable.

13.10: The most workable option is short, frequent quizzes. The frequency will have the effect of increasing overall reliability.

13.11: If the assessment system is based on a scale, such as 90-100 for an A, 80-89 for a B, etc., it is criterion referenced. If the teacher used a distribution and assigns As, Bs, Cs, etc., on the basis of the distribution, it is a norm-referenced system. The former assigns grades on the basis of preset criteria, the latter based on comparisons of students to each other.

13.12: Informal measurements are not systematic, and they are highly unreliable.

13.13: It is easier to assess skills using performance assessments than other types of items.

13.14: More of the content in math and science lends itself to problem solving—a common task that goes beyond the knowledge level—than does the content in other areas, so it is easier for teachers to write items involving problem solving in these areas. Creating test items involving problem solving in American History, for example, is demanding and time consuming for teachers.

13.15: The answer to this question depends on the teacher. Many classes, even at the college and university level, use test items written primarily at the knowledge level.

13.16: The item is invalid, because the students got the incorrect answer for a reason other than not understanding the content. The item can still be reliable, however, because the scoring on the item is consistent. At the very least you should rewrite the item before using it again. On the present test, you could "throw the item out" for purposes of evaluation.

13.17: If they are written clearly and require an *exactly worded* answer, they are objective. However, as soon as answers are allowed to vary and teacher judgment is involved in assessing the quality of the answer, the item becomes subjective.

13.18: The simplest way to fix the item is to rewrite the stem so it reflects one question, such as "Which of the following is part of the circulatory system?" A question about the function of the circulatory system should be a separate item.

13.19: The following represent one way to "fix" these problems:

   1. Which of the following is a function of the circulatory system?
       a. To support the vital organs of the body.
     * b. To transport the blood throughout the body.
       c. To transfer nerve impulses from the brain to the muscles.
       d. To provide for the movement of the body's large muscles.
   2. Of the following, the definition of population density is:
       a. the number of people that live in your city or town.
       b. the number of people that voted in the last presidential election.
     * c. the number of people that live on a certain area of land.
       d. the number of people in cities compared to small towns.
   3. Of the following, the most significant cause of World War II was:
       a. American aid to Great Britain.
       b. Italy's conquering of Ethiopia.
       c. Japan's war on China.
     * d. the devastation of the German economy.
   4. Which of the following is the best description of an insect?
       a. They have one pair of antennae on their head.
     * b. They have three body parts.
       c. They live in water.
       d. They breathe through lungs.
   5. The one of the following is not a reptile is a(n)
       a. alligator
       b. lizard
     * c. frog
       d. turtle
   6. Which of the following illustrates a verb form used as a participle?
       a. He ran quickly to the door.
     * b. I saw a jumping frog contest on TV yesterday.
       c. Thinking is hard for many of us.
       d. To forgive is an admirable trait.

13.20: All of these items are at the knowledge/recall level, a typical problem for true-false items.

13.21: Other content that lends itself to matching includes: 1) dates and events, 2) countries/states and capitals 3) chemical elements and symbols, and 4) literary works and authors.

13.22: Possible items are as follows:

   a) What is the term used to describe a belief, view, or judgment formed about a particular matter?
   b) What is the present day capital of the country of Canada?

13.23: If spelling and grammar were specified in your instructor's criteria, taking off points is valid. If not, taking off points is not valid.

13.24: These are primarily problems with validity. The items are often reliable, but invalid because they are incongruent with goals.

13.25: An example of an authentic assessment would be for Shirley to present a problem such as the following:

   We're having a pizza party. One pizza is cut into 12 pieces, another into 6 pieces, and a third into 4 pieces. Elroy ate one piece from each pizza. How much pizza did he eat altogether?

(Even more authentic would be for the students to actually have a pizza party where pizzas cut into different numbers of slices were served, and having the students determine how much one person or a group of people ate.)

13.26: The item is out of alignment. Being able to state the steps in the scientific method doesn't mean that students "understand" it.

13.27: Products of student efforts are the most common form of alternative assessment at all levels, such as a kindergartner's sheet of written letters, a middle elementary student's art project, a junior high student's science experiment, and a senior high student's persuasive essay. Systematic observation is still uncommon in schools.

13.28: Some products that the portfolio would include could be student responses to math facts, responses to word problems based on the book used in the class, and responses to "real world" problems generated either by the teacher or the students.

13.29: A rating scale might appear as follows:

DIRECTIONS: Assess each of the test items using the following dimensions and for each dimension circling a 5 for an excellent performance, 4 for a very good performance, 3 for good performance, 2 for fair, and 1 for poor.

5 4 3 2 1   States one clear problem in the stem.
5 4 3 2 1   Each distracter is plausible.
5 4 3 2 1   Wording in the stem and correct choice is dissimilar.
5 4 3 2 1   Phrasing in the correct choice and distracters is similar.
5 4 3 2 1   The correct choice and distracters are similar in length.
5 4 3 2 1   Negative wording is appropriately emphasized.
5 4 3 2 1   All distracters have different meanings.

13.30: Constructing a table of specifications before instruction has the advantage of helping to focus instruction. The disadvantage is that instructional adaptations would not be reflected in the table of specifications, so students' understanding of the content covered in the changes would probably not be measured. A table constructed after instruction would likely reflect adaptations, but it wouldn't help the teacher in making decisions about goals and emphasis.

13.31: She is partially consistent. Her procedure ensures that every objective is measured, but a table of specifications also specifies the number of items or emphasis given to each topic as well as the level of the item. Based on the evidence we have, she is giving all objectives equal emphasis, and we know nothing about the levels of her items.

13.32: This answer is highly individual. You probably learned the skills on your own based on your experience in taking tests. (It is unlikely that you had teachers who taught you test-taking skills.)

13.33: As Tanya discussed the upcoming test she did the following: 1) reminded students to read directions, 2) encouraged students to go on if they got stuck, and 3) reminded them to go back to reconsider the ones they skipped.

13.34: Each of these would be adversely affected but for different reasons. To help reduce the problems the teacher might do one or more of the following: 1) schedule plenty of time for the test, 2) carefully monitor the test, and read parts of items for students who are unable to read them on their own, and 3) assign a reader for ESL students.

13.35: In addition to the specific suggestions in the text you might: 1) put three or four questions/problems at the beginning of your tests that all the students are virtually guaranteed to answer correctly; 2) have the test-anxious student come in after school and then give her some practice problems/questions that use the same format as you will use on the actual test. (As she works on the practice items, make encouraging statements to her); 3) talk to her parents or other caregivers and strongly encourage them to take performance pressure off her; and 4) carefully monitor her work (without making it obvious) and drop a gentle hint if you see her beginning to panic. If you believe her anxiety is a danger to her emotional health, you should contact the school counselor and seek his or her advice about the problem?

13.36: Test preparation practices vary. Perhaps the instructor has given you some sample test items to practice on, maybe has described the test content, and could have referred you to additional resources, such as the application exercises in the *Student Study Guide*. Typically this has the effect of reducing test anxiety.

13.37: First, the teacher should schedule ample time for the students to take the test. Then, one reminder about 15 or 20 minutes before the time expires would be appropriate. Continuous reminders will likely have the effect of increasing test anxiety, particularly if students are having difficulty finishing in the allotted time.

13.38: From a behaviorist point of view, positive results serve as reinforcers; from a humanist perspective knowledge of positive results are indicators of personal growth; knowledge of results—either positive or negative—allow learners to explain why they performed the way they did, which according to cognitive theorists is an innate need.

13.39: Arrange for a conference with the parent, and when the person arrives give her or him a written document that describes in detail the exact procedures that you followed in making the alternative assessment and the criteria you used. Then precisely describe the student's performance using the document as a basis. If this fails to convince the parent, solicit the help of your principal.

13.40: Research indicates that graded—versus ungraded—homework has a positive influence on learning. First, talk to the students about copying, reminding them that copying will result in less learning and lower test scores. Then, base at least some portion of your tests on the homework, and in discussing the test point out the link.

13.41: The answers to this question will vary. If the situation you're in is typical, the bulk of your grade will come from tests, quizzes, and projects. Few instructors at the university level give homework assignments.

13.42: Typically, formative evaluation is most valuable for young, at-risk and low-ability students because research indicates that these students' metacognition is less well developed than their counterparts, and they have problems monitoring and regulating their own learning progress.

13.43: The answers to this question will vary. If the situation you're in is typical, it will involve a point system. Most university faculty are quite clear about their grading systems.

13.44: As items are stored in the computer they can be classified in terms of content area and level. Then, when the items are retrieved, they can be accurately placed in the table of specifications.

13.45: The first four items—and particularly the first two—were purposely designed to be easy to minimize test anxiety and to allow students to "get going" on the test. When constructing tests, this is generally good practice.

13.46: While controversial, evidence indicates that testing increases learning. If standardized testing were eliminated, the likely long-range effect would be a reduction in the level of student learning.

13.47: Internship (student teaching) is the most widespread alternative assessment that exists in the preparation of teachers. All types of clinical work, such as in nursing, are forms of alternative assessment. Contests for music and marching bands are additional examples. They are "standardized" to the extent that a panel of judges assesses performance against preset criteria.

13.48: Because the second class is more homogeneous, it would likely be the easier of the two to teach.

13.49: The "statistics" are the mean, median, mode, range, and standard deviation. They help us "describe" a given population or class.

13.50: While many examples exist, the following is one illustration with a class of 30 on a 50-item test. Here we see a median of 38, a mean of 40.5, and a mode of 49. Here we see the uncommon mix of about a third very high achievers with the rest of the class being low achievers. With a limited range of possibilities—scores from 0 to 50—the mean and median cannot vary too much. In contrast, if most people earn $30,000 a year, for example, but a few earn several million, the median and mean can vary dramatically.

```
                                         x
                                         x  x
                                         x  x
                                         x  x
            x  x  x  x  x  x                 x  x
         x  x  x  x  x  x  x  x  x  x  x      x  x
        29 30 31 32 33 34 35 36 37 38 39 40 41 42 43 44 45 46 47 48 49 50
```

13.51: Either mean or median would be acceptable responses. Range and standard deviation are measures of "spread," and mode, mean, and median are measures of central tendency.

13.52: The height represents frequency, such as the number of people at a certain height, or the number getting a certain score. Heights or scores, for example, are represented along the horizontal axis.

13.53: The second class is more like a normal distribution than is the first class, because the mean and median are the same, and the spread of scores more nearly approximates the spread of a normal distribution.

13.54: There is a greater difference between the performances of Jessie and Marsha than there is between Marsha and Al. Students who score at the extremes in terms of percentiles vary more from their counterparts than those who score near the middle of the distribution.

13.55: In the first class with a standard deviation of 4.8, a score of 47 would be in stanine 7 (slightly more than one standard deviation above the mean). In the second distribution with a standard deviation of 3.1, a score of 47 would be in stanine 8 (over one and a half standard deviations above the mean).

13.56: His score was the same as the average score obtained by a student in the fifth month of the fifth grade. It means that the fourth grader is somewhat advanced. (It does not mean that the student should be in the fifth grade, nor does it mean that the student is generally capable of doing fifth grade work.)

13.57: A score of 500 would be at the 50th percentile, and a score of 550 would be one-half a standard deviation above the mean; approximately the 70th percentile.

13.58: A score of 45 would then be 1 standard deviation above the mean, which would be a z-score of 1 and a T-score of 60 (since the mean is defined as 50 and the standard deviation is defined as 10).

13.59: First, diagnostic tests focus primarily on basic skill areas, such as math, reading, and language arts, while achievement tests measure understanding in a wider variety of areas. Second, diagnostic tests include more items that specifically measure student performance in each of the basic skill areas.

13.60: Binet selected school-related skills, such as vocabulary and arithmetic. Since the test included no items measuring artistic creativity or physical coordination, it wouldn't have been useful for that purpose.

13.61: The child's IQ would be 80.

13.62: Renormed means that the test was readministered to a new comparative sample of students. In order to reflect the nation's population, the "norming" group should have the same proportion of minorities as the nation as a whole.

13.63: The two tests both have verbal and performance subtests. They have closely related views of intelligence and they are highly correlated.

13.64: Several factors make group intelligence tests inappropriate for young children—their heavy reliance on reading, the narrow range of tasks, and their inability to adjust for factors such as fatigue, anxiety, or confusion.

13.65: At least two factors are probably operating. First, as research indicates, teachers lack confidence in their own ability to accurately assess student learning, and second, classroom teachers are likely to perceive standardized tests as more accurate and valid than they really are.

13.66: Aptitude is generally considered to be a subset of intelligence. It is the "capacity to acquire knowledge" dimension.

13.67: An achievement test would be used to compare the amount you've learned compared to other classes around the country. A test—used for the purpose of adjusting instruction—which focuses on specific concepts would be a diagnostic test.

13.68: Minimum competency tests are most like achievement tests. They are intended to measure minimum student achievement.

13.69: The advantages in leaving promotion and graduation decisions up to individual teachers—which, since promotion and graduation commonly depend on the grades individual teachers award, is the system in widespread use right now—is that they have the most intimate knowledge of student performance. The disadvantage is that individual teacher assessments vary dramatically, so the process on a widespread basis is unreliable.

13.70: Content bias is more a problem with validity than reliability. If students with limited English proficiency miss an item involving math because they don't know the meaning of a word, for example, the item measures vocabulary instead of math, making the item incongruent with the measurement goal.

13.71: Teachers can do at least three things to help reduce procedural bias. First, try to create a classroom climate where the students perceive the teacher as supportive and caring, the climate is cooperative rather than competitive, and the learning environment is learning focused rather than performance focused (as was discussed in chapter 9). This will help the students take learning and testing seriously. Second, be certain that goals, instruction, and assessment are aligned, and third, give students ample practice in responding to practice test items in test-like conditions.

13.72: The simplest thing a teacher can do is have one or two colleagues read the items and give feedback about possible ambiguity or inappropriate background expectations. Teachers should carefully go over any frequently missed items with the students and listen to their reasons for the answers they gave. Then, rewrite the items to make them clearer.

13.73: To minimize confusion first be certain that directions are simple and clear. Second, encourage students to raise their hands and ask for clarification during the test if they're confused. Third, carefully monitor the students as they work, looking for evidence of confusion.

13.74: Multiple-trait scoring most strongly relates to establishing criteria for rating individual dimensions of a performance assessment.

13.75: Answers to this question depend on the instructor, so they vary. Ambiguity relates to information processing, which we know strongly depends on the perception of the individual. Perception depends on experience (and expectations), and cultural experiences vary widely.

13.76: Social adaptability is an important "life skill." (It relates to Gardner's *interpersonal* intelligence.) Medical history provides information about health factors that could influence cognitive performance, and nonverbal scores can provide information that couldn't be obtained from a student with limited background in English.

13.77: The advantage of a clinical approach is that it allows observers to gather a great deal of very specific information about the learner. The disadvantage, as with many other forms of alternative assessment, is the approach can be unreliable.

Part III
Practice Test Questions

Chapter 2

Use the following information to answer items 1 and 2.

Mrs. Park has taught her students the process of subtracting one- digit from two-digit numbers without regrouping and is now teaching them subtraction with regrouping. Jimmy, a boy big for his age from a upper-income family, is having trouble with the process, however. When given the problems

$$
\begin{array}{cc}
64 & 32 \\
-7 \quad \text{and} & -5 \quad \text{Jimmy gets 63 and 33 as results.}
\end{array}
$$

1. Of the following, the Piagetian concept most closely related to Jimmy's tendency is:
   a. accommodation.
   b. centration.
   c. reversibility.
   d. maturation.
2. Of the following the best explanation for why Jimmy got 63 and 33 as answers is:
   a. Jimmy is accommodating his subtraction without regrouping schema to the new problems.
   b. Jimmy's maturation isn't advanced enough to allow him to solve problems with regrouping.
   c. Jimmy is reversing the process from problems with regrouping to problems without regrouping.
   d. Jimmy remained at equilibrium by getting the results that he did.

3. You're teaching the concept of noun to your third grade students. Using Piaget's theory as a basis for making your decision, the best example of the following to use in illustrating the concept would be:
   a. a soccer ball.
   b. a drawing of a house.
   c. a colored picture of an oak tree.
   d. a picture of a girl with the word "girl" written underneath it.

Use the following case study to help in answering items 4-6.

Mr. Kenna's chemistry students are having a difficult time understanding how a solid and a liquid can be at the same temperature when the material is the same (such as an ice cube turning to water). Mr. Kenna explains that it takes energy to change the "state" from solid to liquid without changing the temperature. This change in state is the result of changing the arrangement of the molecules from a solid to a liquid and it takes heat to do that. The kids still don't get it. Based on Piaget's work, which of the following is the best explanation for the students' difficulty?

4. a. The students are not yet chronologically at the age of formal operations and this is a formal operational task.
   b. The students' maturation isn't to the point where they are ready to handle this topic.
   c. The students are among the 50% who don't reach the stage of formal operations.
   d. The students lack the concrete experiences needed to understand the ideas involved.
5. Of the following, the best solution to Mr. Kenna's problem according to Piaget would be to:
   a. describe the process of the change in molecular motion between a solid and a liquid in more detail, so they see the difference.
   b. show them a model illustrating the molecular motion of the substance in each state and the change in motion as it melts.

c. melt a piece of ice in front of them and have them describe it as it melts.

d. have them explain their ideas about melting (instead of describing the process for them).

6. Of the following four concepts the one conceptually least related to the other three in Piaget's theory is:
   a. accommodation.
   b. assimilation.
   c. schema.
   d. adaptation.

Jackie puts a pencil and ruler together because they are both straight.

7. The stage of development that this behavior best illustrates is:
   a. sensori-motor.
   b. preoperational.
   c. concrete operational.
   d. formal operational.
8. The characteristic Jackie is demonstrating is:
   a. identifying cause-effect relationships.
   b. grouping on the basis of a functional relationship.
   c. seriation of objects.
   d. grouping on the basis of a perceptual feature.

Ron, 24, is in a conversation with his fiancee, Kathy. "What are you doing?" Kathy queries. "I want to give the boss a call to see what he thinks of this."

"It bothers me when you do that all the time," Kathy responds. "You're so capable. Why do you want him looking over your shoulder all the time? It hurts me to see you operate like this."

"Don't worry about it, Kat. I know what kind of a guy I am and how I operate best. And, it seems to be working. My last raise was a good one."

9. Based on Erikson's work and the information in the case study, which of the following would Kathy conclude Ron has *least* well resolved?
   a. Trust vs. distrust
   b. Autonomy vs. shame and doubt
   c. Industry vs. inferiority
   d. Identity vs. confusion
10. Based on the information in the case study, which crisis has Ron best resolved?
    a. Trust vs. distrust
    b. Autonomy vs. shame and doubt
    c. Industry vs. inferiority
    d. Identity vs. confusion

11. Mrs. Hanson is a teacher making an effort to apply Erikson's theory to classroom practice. Whenever the opportunity arises in a social studies lesson to discuss prominent figures and their accomplishments, she discusses them thoroughly in an effort to present them as models for the students. Based on this information, which of the following would be the best prediction of Mrs. Hanson's students' ages?
    a. 6
    b. 10
    c. 13
    d. 21

12. Cliff is very self-accepting. He acknowledges his assets and limitations. He takes people at face value and in a reflective mood says, "Well, I've done pretty well. Anyway, I did my best, and

that's all anyone can ask." Of the following, Cliff best fits which stage according to Erikson's theory?
   a. Identity vs. confusion
   b. Intimacy vs. isolation
   c. Generativity vs. stagnation
   d. Integrity vs. despair

13. We've heard of the moral ethic "Don't bite the hand that feeds you." This notion best fits which one of Kohlberg's Stages?
   a. 1
   b. 2
   c. 3
   d. 4

14. Joey tends to be a bit of a bully on the playground, shoving the smaller boys down and making them cry. You take him aside and say, "Joey, how do you think the other kids feel when you treat them like this?" together with other related statements. Amazingly, this seems to help, and Joey's behavior has improved. In the absence of any other information, based on this anecdote, we would judge Joey's age to be no younger than which of the following?
   a. 4
   b. 9
   c. 12
   d. 16

In the following case study identify the stage of moral reasoning best illustrated by each of the numbered paragraphs.

A group of people were sitting at a party discussing tax time with the same concerns people have at that time of the year.
   "I'm taking a trip this summer," Nick declared with a wry grin. "I plan to see my brother. He's a teacher too. We are really going to talk teaching. In fact my kids are going to talk teaching.
   "My trip is going to cost only 65% of what it would have," he finished with a sly look.
(15) "You talk tough now," Judy replied seriously. "You won't be cute when you get audited."
(16) "Well, my brother and I are very close emotionally, my folks are getting older, they'll be there, and they really want to see the kids," Nick responded.
(17) "Shoot, I'd do it in a second," John added. "Besides, everyone does it, and no one would react to your little indiscretion."
(18) "On the other hand," Frances responded pensively. "Nick is technically breaking the law."
   "Ahh, you're a lawyer," Betty responded with a tongue-in-cheek sneer.
(19) "True," Frances responded, though not defensively. "Change the law and I'll go along with it. A more considered group than we made the decision to start with."
   "It's a bad law and a piece of crap," Sharon responded emotionally.
(20) "Well, we can't just go around doing as we please," Tony added cautiously. "I mean what would the world be like if everyone thought like Sharon does. It would be chaos."
   "I'm sorry I brought it up," Nick said with a placating grin.

Chapter 3

Use the following case study to help in answering items 1-5.

Mrs. Wilson breaks her first graders into groups of three and gives each group 12 plastic cubes and a container the cubes will fit into (2 × 2 × 3). They identify the pieces as *cubes* and conclude that they're all the same size. She has them put cubes into the container. They remove the cubes and she asks them how much space the cubes took up, and leads them to conclude "12 cubes." She asks them what they call the space, and when they're unable to say "Volume," she tells them they have a *volume* of "twelve cubes." To reinforce the idea, she then asks them what the *volumes* of their boxes are, and leads them to say "twelve cubes."

1. Based on this information which of the following is the best evaluation of Mrs. Wilson's teaching of the concept *volume?*
   a. Her instruction was effective because the students had a concrete illustrations of *cube.*
   b. Her instruction was effective because she reinforced the concept by having them say they had a volume of "twelve cubes."
   c. Her instruction was ineffective, because she should have used actual units (such as twelve cubic inches) instead of "twelve cubes."
   d. Her instruction was ineffective, because she shouldn't have *told* them they had an *volume* of twelve cubes.

2. Consider the students' understanding of *cube* compared to their understanding of *volume.* Which of the following is the most valid description of their understanding?
   a. Their understanding of *cube* and *volume* will be similar, since they saw concrete examples of each.
   b. Their understanding of *volume* will be more complete than their understanding of *cube,* since the lesson focused on volume.
   c. Their understanding of *volume* will be more complete than their understanding of *cube* since Mrs. Solomon reinforced the idea at the end.
   d. Their understanding of *cube* will be more complete than their understanding of *volume,* since *volume* requires concrete operations and *cube* doesn't.

3. The next day Mrs. Wilson has her students again make a stack of blocks ($2 \times 2 \times 3$) and count the cubes, and she then has them make another one ($1 \times 2 \times 6$) by putting the blocks in two rows of 6, side by side. They again count the cubes. She then asks them if the two volumes are the same or if they are different. Which of the following is the most likely response?
   a. The students will conclude that the volumes are the same, since they can see 12 cubes in each case.
   b. The students will conclude that the volumes are the same since they actually counted the cubes.
   c. The students will conclude that the volumes are different, since their understanding of *volume* is likely to be incomplete.
   d. The students will conclude that the volumes are different, since they look different.

4. Suppose Mr. Johnson, a fourth grade teacher in the same school, did exactly the same thing Mrs. Wilson did—first teaching the concept of *volume* and then in making a $2 \times 2 \times 3$ solid and then a $1 \times 2 \times 6$ solid. He asks them if the two volumes are the same or if they are different? Which of the following is the most likely response?
   a. The students will conclude that the volumes are the same, since they can see 12 cubes in each case.
   b. The students will conclude that volumes are the same since fourth graders are chronologically at the age of concrete operations.
   c. The students will conclude that the volumes are different, since their understanding of *volume* is likely to be incomplete.
   d. The students will conclude that the volumes are different, since they look different.

5. Suppose you were a fifth grade teacher and you wanted to teach the concept of *volume,* and you also wanted the students to understand the units for volume, such as cubic inches. Which of the following is the most developmentally valid approach to reaching these goals, based on the thinking patterns of fifth graders?
   a. Use the same approach as Mrs. Wilson and Mr. Johnson did, then have them measure the cubes, and then lead them to the units.
   b. First have them measure the cubes, and have them state that the volume is one cubic inch. Then do essentially what Mrs. Wilson and Mr. Johnson did.

c. First state that one of the units for volume is "cubic inches" and then have them solve problems with solid shapes of different dimensions.

d. First tell the students that one of the units for volume is cubic inches. Then have them measure the cubes, and then have them solve problems with solid shapes of different dimensions.

Use the following case study to answer items 6-8.

The second grade team at Crystal Lake Elementary school is trying to increase their second graders understanding of the need to pay attention.

Mr. Winthrop says to his students, "Now listen everyone. It is very important to pay attention, so that we can all learn more. We pay attention when we look at a person when the person is talking, or we look at the board when I point to it." He reminds the students about the need for attention every day.

Mrs. Grimley says to her students, "Attention is very important. Let's see what we mean by attention," and she had Mrs. Myers, a parent volunteer, talk to her while she kept her eyes focused on Mrs. Myers's face as Mrs. Myers talked. Mrs. Grimley then makes comments such as, "Jeanna is doing a very good job of paying attention," whenever she sees them demonstrating attentive behaviors.

Mr. Minchew has a rule that says, "Pay attention at all times when the teacher is talking." When students don't pay attention, he first reminds them, and after three infractions, they're isolated from the class.

Mrs. Patterson makes comments, such as, "David has been very attentive for this whole lesson. He has kept his eyes focused on the front of the all the time while I've been talking. That's excellent," whenever she sees students who are particularly attentive.

6. Based on research, the teacher's approach likely to be <u>most</u> successful is:
   a. Mr. Winthrop
   b. Mrs. Grimley
   c. Mr. Minchew
   d. Mrs. Patterson

7. Based on research, the teacher's approach likely to be <u>second most</u> successful is:
   a. Mr. Winthrop
   b. Mrs. Grimley
   c. Mr. Minchew
   d. Mrs. Patterson

8. Based on research, the teacher's approach likely to be <u>least</u> successful is:
   a. Mr. Winthrop
   b. Mrs. Grimley
   c. Mr. Minchew
   d. Mrs. Patterson

9. Four teachers were having coffee one day after school, and as their conversation went on, they began talking about the low self-esteem of some of their disadvantaged students, particularly with respect to academic work. They then began to discuss the different ways that the students' academic self-concepts could be improved. As they were talking, Mrs. Ivanisevich commented, "I try to give my students some independence, and I let them help me decide on the learning activities that we're going to conduct."

Mr. Lilyquist added, "I try to provide an environment where the students know I care for and trust them."

Mr. Henderson continued, "I try to attack the problem formally. I have a series of activities in which we discuss how important it is to feel good about ourselves. The activities help the students to see that they're all worthwhile people and valuable to the world."

Mrs. Gomez countered, "I think the primary thing is that the students accomplish something, so I try to be sure that they're successful on the learning activities we do. Then they feel good about what they've accomplished."

Based on research and these descriptions, the teacher most likely to be successful is:

a. Mrs. Ivanisevich
b. Mr. Lilyquist
c. Mr. Henderson
d. Mrs. Gomez

Use the following case study to answer items 10 and 11.

In your class of 9th graders you have four students who characterize the wide range of physical development in teenagers. Miguel has the physique of an athlete, and is shaving nearly every day. Christina is also physically mature; she's nearly 5'8" tall and has a young woman's body. Alexandra and Tom are at the other end of the spectrum; they both look like 6th graders.

10. If the impact of their development fits patterns typical for adolescents, which of the following is the most accurate prediction.
   a. Miguel and Christina will likely be more poised, relaxed, and outgoing than will Alexandra and Tom.
   b. Christina will likely be more poised, relaxed, and outgoing than will Alexandra, but Miguel will likely be less self-confident, more rebellious, and more dependent than will Tom.
   c. Miguel will likely be more poised, relaxed, and outgoing than will Tom, but Christina will likely be less outgoing, less sociable, and more shy than will Alexandra.
   d. Alexandra and Tom both will likely be more poised, relaxed and outgoing than will Miguel and Christina.

11. In terms of developmental differences' long-range impact, which of the following is the most accurate description.
   a. The negative effects are likely to be mild for all four students.
   b. The potential negative effects will be greater for Tom and Christina than they are for Miguel and Alexandra.
   c. The potential long-term negative effects are likely to be quite severe for both Tom and Alexandra.
   d. The potential negative effects are likely to linger for Christina but will be quite mild for the other three students.

12. Joan and Andy are pre-kindergartners. If the children are consistent with patterns of development identified by research, which of the following would be the most valid prediction?
   a. Joan's verbal ability will be superior to Andy's.
   b. Andy's verbal ability will be superior to Joan's.
   c. Their verbal abilities will be about equal.
   d. No prediction of verbal ability differences can be made as early as pre-kindergarten.

Chapter 4

Use the following case study to answer items 1-4.

Gabriella is a fourth grader at Oakridge Elementary School—a school populated mostly by children from upper middle class families. Gabriella, whose native language is Spanish, lives with her divorced mother—a minimum wage housekeeper who left school after the 10th grade. Gabriella has a limited background. In a discussion of American westward expansion, for example, she asked what a bridle was, as Mrs. Petschonek talked about the gear the cowboys used. Also, she had never heard of the country Hungary, confusing it with being hungry. However, Gabriella learns new ideas in class more quickly than many of her classmates, and she periodically asks questions atypical of fourth graders, such as, "Why are there so many movies about cowboys if there weren't really that many of them?"

1. Based on the information in the case study, which of the following is the best prediction?
    a. Gabriella will get a lower score than will her typical peers on some sections of typical intelligence tests.
    b. Gabriella will score about the same as typical fourth graders on most sections of typical intelligence tests.
    c. Gabriella will score higher than typical fourth graders on most sections of typical intelligence tests.
    d. We can't make any predictions about Gabriella's performance on intelligence tests based on the information in the case study.

2. Based on the information in the case study and researchers' conceptions of intelligence, which of the following is the best description?
    a. Gabriella is less intelligent than most of her peers.
    b. Gabriella's intelligence is about comparable to that of her peers.
    c. Gabriella is more intelligent than most of her peers.
    d. We don't have any evidence one way or the other about Gabriella's intelligence based on the information in the case study.

3. Based on the information in the case study, of the following, which is the best conclusion we can make about Gabriella's socioeconomic status?
    a. It is lower than that of her peers.
    b. It is about the same as that of her peers.
    c. It is higher than that of her peers.
    d. We don't have enough information from the case study to make a conclusion about Gabriella's socioeconomic status.

4. Based on information in the case study and research on school dropouts, if Gabriella fits typical patterns for students with her background and socioeconomic status, which of the following is the best prediction?
    a. She is much less likely to drop out of school than is a typical classmate.
    b. She is slightly less likely to drop out than is a typical classmate.
    c. The likelihood of Gabriella dropping out is about the same as that of a typical classmate.
    d. Gabriella is about twice as likely to drop out as is a typical classmate.

5. We have all met people that seem to be very adept at getting along with other people, even though our perception is that they are only modestly "bright." Based on our study of individual differences, the best description of this phenomenon is:
    a. Even though people are not intelligent, they can have good social skills.
    b. Interpersonal skills is one dimension of intelligence according to Gardner.
    c. Interpersonal skills is part of the processing component of Sternberg's triarchic theory of intelligence.
    d. Human relations is part of the abstract thinking and reasoning part of general descriptions of intelligence.

Use the following information for items 6 and 7.

Joe and Adam are students who have nearly identical scores on tests of reading ability, and the self-esteem of the two boys is about the same. Their test scores are similar to those of students who are placed in low-ability classes. Joe is then placed in a low-ability fifth grade class for reading, while Adam is somehow placed in a class with students of average and slightly above average ability.

6. If the boys' achievement at the end of the year is typical of patterns identified by research, which of the following statements is the most accurate prediction?
    a. Their achievement will be about the same, since they have nearly identical scores on tests of ability.

b. Joe will achieve higher than will Adam, since he is in a class that best fits his ability level.

c. Adam will achieve higher than will Joe because of the composition of the class and the teacher's expectations.

d. We can't make any conclusions about the boys' achievement based on the classes in which they're placed.

7. Consider the effects of the two boys' placements on their self-esteem. If the effects are consistent with patterns identified by research, which of the following is the best prediction?

a. Joe's self-esteem will be higher than Adam's since he is with students of similar ability, while Adam is in with students whose abilities are higher than his.

b. Joe's self-esteem will be higher than Adam's since he is likely to experience more success in his class than Adam is in his.

c. Adam's self-esteem will be higher than Joe's because being placed in low-ability classes detracts from self-esteem.

d. The self-esteem of the two boys will remain about the same, because class placement has little effect on self-esteem.

Use the following information for items 8 and 9.

In her class of 27 students, Verna Maxwell has 14 students who are cultural minorities. Among them are Henry, a Native American, Kim, a Cambodian refugee, Lu, a second-generation Chinese American, and Rom, who has recently moved to American from India.

8. Based on Ogbu's work, which of the four is most likely to experience *cultural inversion?*

a. Henry

b. Kim

c. Lu

d. Rom

9. In working with her cultural minorities in question and answer activities, which of the following is the best advice we can give Verna?

a. Call on the minority students only when they volunteer, because we many not understand their preferred learning styles.

b. Call on students such as Henry and Lu, because they are Americans, but don't direct questions to Kim and Rom, because they may not be comfortable in an American classroom.

c. Use typical questioning patterns with Henry and Lu, but ask Kim and Rom open-ended questions.

d. Treat all the students, including the cultural minorities, as equally as possible in both the type and number of questions asked.

Use the following case study to answer items 10-12.

Mrs. Parker has 14 girls and 15 boys in her fifth grade class. She says, "The Battle of Gettysburg is believed to be the turning point of the Civil War. In what state is Gettysburg?" Then she asks, "What do you suppose would have happened if the South had won the battle instead of the North?"

10. If Mrs. Parker's questioning is typical of the *types* of questions directed to boys and girls, which of the following is most likely?

a. She will direct both her questions to girls.

b. She will direct both her questions to boys.

c. She will direct the first question to a girl and the second question to a boy.

d. She will direct the first question to a boy and the second question to a girl.

e. There will be no pattern in her questioning behavior.

11. If Mrs. Parker's questioning is typical of the *number* of questions addressed to boys and girls, which of the following is most likely?

a. She will direct more questions to boys.

b. She will direct more questions to girls.

c. She will direct about the same number of questions to boys as to girls.

12. Look again at the case study describing Gabriella and her situation. Is she an at-risk student? Explain. What should her teacher do to best help Gabriella succeed in school?

Chapter 5

Use the following case study to answer items 1-5.

Mr. Griffin, a 5th grade teacher, in observing Samone Duvalier, one of his students—originally from Haiti—thinks that Samone may have a specific learning disability. Samone, a native French speaking child who speaks competent English, is given the WISC-III, an individually administered intelligence test (in English) by certified special education officials. He scores very low on the vocabulary section of the test compared to the other sections, and he is diagnosed as having a specific learning disability. Mr. Griffin and exceptional student specialists from the school prepare and implement an IEP. Part of the IEP calls for Samone being placed in a resource reading program for one hour a day. (He is mainstreamed the rest of the day.) Mrs. Duvalier, Samone's mother, after meeting with the school officials, objects to the placement, and asks for Samone's school records and test results. The school offers the name of a person who could do an independent evaluation of Samone but will not release their own test results, only saying that Samone's score was very low in the vocabulary section.

1. According to PL 94-142, the school's refusal to release the records was:
   a. against the law, because of the provision guaranteeing parental involvement.
   b. against the law, because of the provision guaranteeing minority protection, since Samone is a cultural minority.
   c. within the law since Samone was found to have a disability. It would have been against the law if no disability was found.
   d. within the law since Samone was mainstreamed for most of the school day (only in a resource program for an hour a day.)

2. The school officials violated a specific provision of PL 94-142 in their handling of Samone's case. Of the following, the best description of the violation is:
   a. placing Samone in a resource reading program.
   b. officials offering the name of an independent evaluator.
   c. mainstreaming Samone for most of the day.
   d. giving Samone the test in English.

3. Consider the school officials' use of the WISC-III as a basis for making their assessment of Samone. Based on PL 94-142, which of the following is the most accurate statement?
   a. Officials' use of the test was within the law, since the WISC-III is validated and widely used.
   b. Officials' use of the WISC-III was *not* within the law since it is an intelligence test.
   c. Officials' use of the WISC-III was within the law, but should have been supplemented with another measure before Samone was placed in the resource program.
   d. The use of the WISC-III was within the law, since the test was given by certified personnel.

4. Consider the school officials' offering of an independent evaluator to diagnose Samone's possible exceptionality. Based on PL 94-142, which of the following is the most accurate statement?
   a. The offer was within the law.
   b. The offer is prohibited by the law.
   c. The law doesn't speak to the offer of an independent evaluation.

5. Consider the development and implementation of Samone's IEP. Based on PL 94-142, which of the following is the most accurate statement?
   a. The development and implementation of the IEP was done according to the law.
   b. The development of the IEP was against the law, since Mr. Griffin—a regular teacher rather than a certified special education expert—was involved in the process.

c. The development and implementation of the IEP was against the law, since it called for Samone being removed from the regular classroom for part of the day.

d. The development and implementation of the IEP was against the law, since Samone's mother didn't sign it.

6. Alfredo, an Hispanic student and Ken, a white student in Mrs. Evans 4th grade class both do very good work. Alfredo, although a bit sloppy in some of his homework, has a great imagination, and often makes comments in class discussions of problems and issues that indicates an uncommon level of reflection in a 4th grader. He can even be slightly disruptive, although not really a management problem. Ken, on the other hand, is every teacher's ideal. He follows directions, his work is extremely neat, and he is never a management problem. Ken and Alfredo scored similarly on achievement tests in the 3rd grade.

Based on this information, if Mrs. Evans's class is consistent with patterns identified by research, which of the following is most likely?

a. Ken is more likely to be identified as gifted than is Alfredo.
b. Alfredo is more likely to be identified as gifted than is Ken.
c. Ken and Alfredo are equally likely to be identified as gifted.
d. Neither Ken nor Alfredo are likely to be identified as gifted, since we have no evidence that either has taken an intelligence test.

7. Which of the following are classified as students with exceptionalities?

1. Students who have an intellectual handicap
2. Students who have specific learning disabilities
3. Students who have behavioral disorders (emotional handicaps)
4. Students who are gifted and talented
5. Students who have hearing and visual impairments

a. 1,2,3,4,5
b. 1,2,3,5
c. 1,2,5
d. 2,3,5
e. 1,2

8. Donna and John are two students in your second grade class. If they are consistent with patterns identified by research, which of the following is the most accurate statement?

a. Donna and John are about *equally* likely to be diagnosed as having ADD-H (attention deficit disorder with hyperactivity).
b. Donna is *slightly* more likely than John to be diagnosed as having ADD-H.
c. Donna is *much* (three to nine times) more likely than John to be diagnosed as having ADD-H.
d. John is *slightly* more likely than Donna to be diagnosed as having ADD-H.
e. John is *much* (three to nine times) more likely than Donna to be diagnosed as having ADD-H.

Chapter 6

Use the following case study to help in answering items 1 and 2.

Tim is in kindergarten. His mother takes him to school. Tim is happy when his mother is there but is upset when she leaves. Mr. Soo begins to talk and joke with Tim while his mother is there, and now Tim is satisfied when his mother leaves.

Consider this situation to be a case of classical conditioning.

1. The conditioned stimulus would be:
    a. the school.
    b. Mr. Soo talking and joking with Tim.
    c. Tim's mother.
    d. happiness.
    e. upset.
2. The conditioned response would be:
    a. the school.
    b. happiness.
    c. upset.
    d. satisfaction.
    e. Tim's mother.

Use the following information to answer items 3 and 4.

Martina is very uneasy in anticipating the beginning of her junior high school experience. Sensing her uneasiness, her dad drove her to school the first morning. They have a close relationship, and Martina feels very warm when she's with him.

Martina's dad dropped her off at school, and she and walked uncertainly into her home room. As she came through the door, Mrs. Hafner smiled broadly, put her arm around Martina and said, "Welcome to the school, sweetheart. Your records tell us that you're new here. I know you're going to like it." Martina felt instant relief. Mrs. Hafner proved to be consistent in her manner. Now, as she goes into the school each day, Martina is quite at ease.

3. The best illustration of the conditioned stimulus would be:
    a. the school.
    b. Mrs. Hafner talking to her and putting her arm around her.
    c. feeling at ease.
    d. feeling instant relief.
4. The conditioned response would be:
    a. the warm feeling she has with her father.
    b. relief.
    c. Mrs. Hafter's manner.
    d. feeling at ease.

5. Mrs. Hafner notices that Jason is very shy in class discussions, so she quietly praises him every time he makes an effort to respond. Jason now seems much more willing to try to answer when she calls on him.
    Her behavior can best be described as:
    a. a continuous schedule of reinforcement.
    b. satiation.
    c. a variable ratio schedule of reinforcement.
    d. negative reinforcement.
    e. shaping.

Use the following information to answer items 6 and 7.

"This test was impossible. They're always so tricky," Mr. Tuff's students complain as he finishes his discussion of a test he had just handed back. "And they're so long," they continue.

Mr. Tuff then consciously makes his next test easier and shorter, hoping his students won't complain so much. He gives the test, scores it, and returns it.

"Not again," some students comment about half way through the discussion of the test. "Yes, you must love to write tricky items," some others add.

Again, in preparing his next test, he reduces the application level of the items and makes the test still shorter.

6. In its impact on Mr. Tuff's behavior, the case study best illustrates:
   a. positive reinforcement.
   b. negative reinforcement.
   c. presentation punishment.
   d. removal punishment.
   e. a conditioned response.
7. In its impact on the students' behavior, the case study best illustrates:
   a. positive reinforcement.
   b. negative reinforcement.
   c. presentation punishment.
   d. removal punishment.
   e. a conditioned response.

8. Mike, the class "toughy" likes to bully the smaller kids by knocking them down and twisting their arms until they say "Give!" Mike caught Jamey on the playground, and though Jamey put up a good struggle, he finally said "Give." It happened again later that week, and after a short tussle Jamey said "Give," as Mike pushed him to the ground. Today Mike started running toward Jamey, and Jamey yelled "Give," before Mike quite got to him.

   In its influence on Jamey's verbal behavior, the example best illustrates:
   a. a conditioned response.
   b. presentation punishment.
   c. removal punishment.
   d. positive reinforcement.
   e. negative reinforcement.

Use the following case study to answer test items 9-12.

Mrs. Batton gets up from her reading group every few minutes to go and circulate among the students who are doing seatwork to offer encouragement.

On one of the occasions where Mrs. Batton is circulating, she comments, "I'm very pleased with the way Jimmy is working so conscientiously on his assignment."

9. Mrs. Batton's behavior best illustrates an application of:
   a. fixed-interval reinforcement.
   b. variable-interval reinforcement.
   c. variable-ratio reinforcement.
   d. vicarious reinforcement.
10. For Jimmy, Mrs. Batton's comment is intended to be:
    a. a fixed-interval reinforcer.
    b. a variable-interval reinforcer.
    c. a positive reinforcer.
    d. a vicarious reinforcer.
11. For the rest of the class, Mrs. Batton's comment is intended to be:
    a. a fixed-interval reinforcer.
    b. a variable-interval reinforcer.
    c. a positive reinforcer.
    d. a vicarious reinforcer.
    e. a negative reinforcer.
12. In this situation, Jimmy's behavior is best described as:
    a. positive reinforcement.
    b. negative reinforcement.
    c. a classically conditioned response.
    d. modeling.
    e. vicarious conditioning.

13. Mrs. Locke has been working with Li, a very shy first grader. Initially, every time Li gave any sort of response in a reading group or class activity, Mrs. Locke praised her liberally. Gradually, Li became more willing to respond. Mrs. Locke then praised her when she took the initiative to respond, and now Li is praised when she gives partially correct answers. Of the following, the best description of Mrs. Locke's technique would be called:
    a. positive reinforcement of desired behaviors.
    b. variable-interval reinforcement of desired behaviors.
    c. continuous-ratio reinforcement of desired behaviors.
    d. shaping of desired behaviors.
    e. conditioned responses.

14. Mrs. Massey gives a short quiz every day in her pre-algebra class. Mr. Parker also gives quizzes in his pre-algebra class, but he gives them on Tuesdays and Thursdays.
    For students who are successful the teachers' practices best illustrate:
    a. continuous reinforcement in Mrs. Massey's class and a fixed-interval reinforcement schedule in Mr. Parker's.
    b. a fixed-ratio reinforcement schedule in Mrs. Massey's class and a fixed-interval schedule in Mr. Parker's.
    c. a fixed-interval schedule in Mrs. Massey's class and a variable-interval schedule in Mr. Parker's.
    d. a fixed-interval schedule in both classes.

15. In a question and answer session, Mr. Hanson says, "Now what is the first step in the problem, Jimmy?"
    ". . . I'm not sure," Jimmy responds after sitting and looking at the problem for several seconds.
    "Help him out, Kelly," Mr. Hanson smiles.
    "We first must find the common denominator," Kelly answers. Later in the lesson, Mr Hanson is examining another problem.
    "OK, now what do we do? Jimmy?"
    "I don't know," Jimmy says after glancing at the problem.
    "Help him out once more, Kelly," Mr. Hanson says supportively.

    a) Explain Jimmy's behavior, identifying the specific concept or concepts from behaviorism that best apply. (Support your statements with evidence from the example.) b) What is Jimmy likely to do the next time he is called on? c) Describe what Mr. Kelly might have done differently that would have been more effective.

Chapter 7

1. Research indicates that teachers who move around the room, make eye contact with students, gesture, and display other related behaviors have students who learn more than teachers who don't demonstrate these behaviors. Of the following, the feature of the information processing model that most closely relates to these behaviors is:
    a. orienting stimulus.
    b. perception.
    c. rehearsal.
    d. encoding.

2. Mr. Tabor is working with his class on direct and indirect objects and displays the following sentence on the overhead.

    As he scrambled to avoid the pass rush, Jack threw Andy a perfect pass.

He then asks, "What do you notice about the sentence?" Of the following, the feature of the information processing model that most closely relates to the question is:
a. attention.
b. perception.
c. elaboration.
d. organization.
e. imagery.

3. Mr. Hunt always follows his presentations in his algebra I class with an assignment where the students practice the skills and ideas he has presented. Research supports the technique of following presentations with student practice. Of the following, the feature of the information processing model that most closely relates to Mr. Hunt's approach is:
a. activity.
b. attention.
c. perception.
d. retrieval.

4. Ben Johnson has had his analytic geometry students working on finding the formulas for parabolas, and is now moving to formulas for ellipses. He starts by reviewing the features of parabolas, such as the focal point, and he then moved to the similar features in ellipses, such as having the students note that they have two focal points. Of the following, the concept from the information processing model that most closely relates to Ben's technique is:
a. discrepant events as attention getters (orienting stimuli), since two focal points compared to one is discrepant.
b. expectations influencing perception. The students don't expect to see two focal points.
c. mnemonic devices to aid encoding.
d. elaboration to aid encoding.
e. activity to aid encoding.

5. The research says that in order to learn concepts most effectively students should be provided with both a definition of the concept and examples of the concept. This research is most closely related in the information processing model to:
a. orienting stimuli.
b. rehearsal.
c. perception.
d. meaningfulness.
e. attention.

Use the following to answer items 6 and 7.

You are using the information processing model as a basis for guiding your instruction and you are teaching your students about direct and indirect objects.

6. Based on the model, which of the following would be the best way to *begin* your lesson?
a. Take a ball out from behind your desk and throw it to one of the students.
b. Ask the students to describe what direct and indirect objects mean to them.
c. Write a sentence on the board and underline the direct and indirect object in it.
d. Tell the students that the topic for the day is direct and indirect objects, and that they will use these parts of speech in their writing.

7. Based on the model, which of the following should you do as the *second* step in your lesson?
a. Ask students questions that will check their understanding of your examples.
b. Have the students rehearse the information you first give them to help retain it in working memory

    c. Devise a means of getting the information into the sensory registers.

    d. Have the students practice the information so it will be encoded into long-term memory.

Use the following information to answer item 8.

Luis Garcia is teaching his 5th graders about the Northern and Southern colonies prior to the Civil War. He prepares a chart, which is outlined as follows:

	Landforms	Climate	Economy	Lifestyle
Northern Colonies				
Southern Colonies				

He assigns teams of two to gather information about each of the cells in the chart (such as the economy in the Northern Colonies). The students provide the information, Luis helps them organize it and they put it in the chart.

8. Luis's use of the chart in his lesson best illustrates which of the following as an attempt to help the students encode the information into long-term memory by making it more meaningful.
    a. Activity
    b. Organization
    c. Elaboration
    d. Perception
    e. Mnemonics

9. A teacher complains, "I stood there for 15 minutes and explained the procedure for solving the problems until I was blue in the face. I know the procedure was a little hard, but this morning they came in and it was as if they had only heard half of what I said. I don't get it." Of the following, the component of the information processing model that most closely relates to this problem is:
    a. perception.
    b. the sensory registers.
    c. working memory.
    d. rehearsal.
    e. long-term memory.

10. The primary purpose in preparing practice exercises such as the ones you're now analyzing is to:
    a. attract and maintain your attention.
    b. be certain that you're perceiving the exercises properly.
    c. be sure that your working memory isn't overloaded when you take a quiz or test.
    d. help you encode this information by putting you in an active role.
    e. give you practice in rehearsing the information we're now studying.

11. Brandon and Giselle are studying for a test. "What are you doing?" Brandon asks.
    "I always write out the answers, rather than simply read the answer given in the book," Giselle responds. "I remember the information better if I do that."
    Of the following, Giselle is most demonstrating:
    a. elaboration.
    b. meta-attention.
    c. proactive facilitation.
    d. metamemory.

For each of the following, mark *S* if the description fits the *sensory registers,* *W* if the description fits *working memory,* and *L* if the description fits *long-term memory.* (The description may fit one, two, or all three memory stores.)

12. Information in it exists in the form of "perceived reality."
13. Has virtually unlimited capacity.
14. Requires the learner's attention in order for information to enter it.
15. Is the store to which the concept of "automaticity" most strongly relates.

Chapter 8

Use the information below to answer items 1-6.

Three teachers were teaching their students the concept *adverb.*

Mrs. Evans told the students that adverbs modify verbs, adjectives, and other adverbs, and went on to say words, such as *quickly, openly, very,* and *rapidly* were adverbs and wrote the words on the board.

Mrs. D'Armas showed the students the sentences:

"Joe quickly jumped into the straight lunch line when Mrs. Smith reminded him."
"Ronnie very openly described his strong feelings about the incident."
"Jim has extra large biceps."

She pointed out that the underlined words were adverbs, and the class determined what they modified. They then formed a definition of adverbs and she wrote it on the board.

Mrs. Voltaire wrote the statement, "Adverbs are parts of speech that modify verbs, adjectives, and other adverbs," on the board and showed the students the following sentences:

"Hank is an extremely smart student."
"Jo powerfully made her argument by stating the facts in the matter."

She then had Susan walk across the floor, and prompted the students to state, "Susan walked quickly across the floor," she wrote the sentence on the board, and she underlined the word *quickly.* She then pointed out that the underlined words in the sentences were adverbs.

1. The type of content the teachers were attempting to teach would best be described as:
   a. discriminations.
   b. concepts.
   c. rules.
   d. declarative knowledge.
   e. cognitive strategies.
2. The students learned Mrs. Voltaire's statement, "Adverbs are parts of speech that modify verbs, adjectives, and other adverbs."
   The type of learning that resulted would most accurately be called:
   a. concepts.
   b. rules.
   c. principles.
   d. declarative knowledge.
3. The students also learned that the *name* of parts of speech that modify verbs, adjectives, and other adverbs is "adverb." The type of learning that this best represents is:
   a. discriminations.
   b. concepts.
   c. rules.
   d. principles.
   e. declarative knowledge.
4. The way that students learn the *names* of concepts is primarily through:
   a. rehearsal.

    b. examples.

    c. organization.

    d. encoding.

5. The next day, Mrs. D'Armas showed the students the sentence:

   Steve is rapidly improving in his work in advanced math.

   She asked the students to identify what *rapidly* was in the sentence. They said, "It's an adverb." The type of learning represented by their answer is best described as:
   a. concepts.
   b. rules.
   c. declarative knowledge.
   d. concepts and rules.
   e. concepts and declarative knowledge.

6. Ken, a student in Mrs. D'Armas' class noted that in each of the sentences the adjective came before the noun that it modified. The type of learning that this best represents is:
   a. discriminations.
   b. concepts.
   c. rules.
   d. principles.
   e. cognitive strategies.

7. Of the following, which is the best example for teaching the concept *adjective?*
   a. The word *big* written on the chalkboard
   b. The statement, "Adjectives modify nouns and pronouns," written on the chalkboard
   c. A picture of a large building with a small building beside it
   d. The sentence, "The <u>heavy</u> truck nearly ran over the <u>small</u> car," written on the chalkboard

8. You want to teach the students "Objects expand when they're heated." If successful, this would result in the students learning:
   a. discriminations.
   b. concepts.
   c. rules.
   d. principles.
   e. generalizations.

9. Of the following, which is the best example for teaching "Objects expand when they're heated"?
   a. Ask the students why they suppose bridges have expansion joints in them.
   b. Ask the students to think about a sidewalk. Prompt them to notice that a sidewalk is not a solid piece of concrete; rather it is in sections. Ask them why they think the sections exist.
   c. Fill two identical balloons with similar amounts of air. Put one in hot water and put the other in ice.
   d. Write the statement, "Objects expand when they're heated," on the board. As the students if they can think of cases where they've seen heated objects expand.

Use the following example for items 10 and 11.

Three students are discussing the use of highlighting as a strategy for making reading from their textbooks more meaningful.

    "I usually highlight the first sentence of nearly every paragraph, because that's supposed to be the topic sentence," Karen comments. "Then I return later and focus on them. Sometimes I'll highlight a different sentence, because it seems to be the most important."

    "I highlight passages that I think are important," Joanne adds. "I look for key terms and lists and stuff. I try not to highlight too much."

"I highlight practically whole chapters," Brad counters. "I read along with it as I'm highlighting. I think it helps."

10. Based on the information in the example, the student whose strategy is likely to be *most* effective is:
    a. Karen
    b. Joanne
    c. Brad

11. Based on the information in the example, the student whose strategy is likely to be *least* effective is:
    a. Karen
    b. Joanne
    c. Brad

12. Think about the three teachers. The one whose students are *most* likely to *transfer* the information is:
    a. Mrs. Evans
    b. Mrs. D'Armas
    c. Mrs. Voltaire

13. The one whose students are *least* likely to *transfer* the information is:
    a. Mrs. Evans
    b. Mrs. D'Armas
    c. Mrs. Voltaire

14. Suppose you want to teach the rule "When making nouns possessive add an apostrophe s if the noun is singular or if the noun is plural and doesn't end in s, and merely add an apostrophe if the noun is plural and ends in s. Create a list of examples that will have the greatest possible likelihood of promoting transfer in your students. Provide a rationale for your list.

Chapter 9

For items 1-6, mark A if the best fits a humanistic view of motivation, mark B, if it fits a behaviorist view, C for a cognitive view, and S for a social learning view.

1. "I try to give my kids' tests back to them the next day. They try harder when they know how they're doing."
2. "Kenny is always seeking attention. I think he has a bad home life, so the attention makes him feel like he's 'in with the guys'."
3. "I needed that grade. When I do well, I feel like trying harder; when I do poorly, I don't feel like trying so hard."
4. "Steve is always acting up. He wouldn't do it except he gets the attention of the other kids in the class."
5. "I try to get the kids to think they're learning something important and challenging. Then, I fix it so they can 'get it,' so they feel 'smart'."
6. "I always try to start my lessons with a problem or something they don't quite expect. It helps keep the kids interested."

7. Janet enjoys living in a large city, because "it gives me a chance to go to a play now and then, a concert, and maybe even the opera." Based on Maslow's work, we would conclude from this information that:
   a. Janet's intellectual achievement need has been satisfied.
   b. Janet is a self-actualized person.

c. Janet feels a sense of belonging with family and/or friends.

d. Janet is compensating for a feeling of low self-esteem.

Use the following example for items 8-12.

Their teacher has returned a test, and the students are commenting on the results.

"I just can't do it," Kathy moaned slapping her test down on her desk after seeing a D on it. "I guess I just can't do French."

Billy nonchalantly shrugged, seeing a D+, "I would have done OK, but I just couldn't get into studying for this one. I never opened my book."

"Weird," Jeff added. "I got a B and I really didn't understand this stuff. I must have been good at guessing or something. I don't know how I did it."

Seeing a C+, Sandra said shaking her head, "I knew this test was going to be really rough, and I just wasn't ready. I will be next time though."

8. The student whose attribution has an external locus of control is:
   a. Kathy.
   b. Billy.
   c. Jeff.
   d. Sandra.

9. The student who is in the greatest danger of developing "learned helplessness" is:
   a. Kathy.
   b. Billy.
   c. Jeff.
   d. Sandra.

10. The student who is most likely to have an incremental view of ability is:
    a. Kathy.
    b. Billy.
    c. Jeff.
    d. Sandra.

11. The student who has the most fragile sense of competence and self worth based on a need to "look smart" is probably:
    a. Kathy.
    b. Billy.
    c. Jeff.
    d. Sandra.

12. The student with the most desirable attribution is:
    a. Kathy.
    b. Billy.
    c. Jeff.
    d. Sandra.

13. Mrs. Kryzewski spends a lot of time with her students both before and after school. The feature of the motivational teaching model that best relates to her tendency to spend extra time is:
    a. enthusiasm.
    b. order and safety.
    c. comprehension.
    d. challenge.
    e. warmth and empathy.

For items 14-16, read the comments made by teachers and then identify the specific *teacher characteristic*, specific *climate variable*, or specific *instructional variable* from the Model for Promoting Student Motivation that is illustrated by each comment.

14. "I have made a commitment to my class," Keith commented. "If I ever do anything that breaks one of our rules or is inconsistent with what I encourage them to do, I've told the class to remind me of it, and we then discuss it as a group."

    _____

15. "I like to use a lot of questioning in my class. I won't ever leave kids who've answered incorrectly until I get acceptable answers from them."

    _____

16. "When I give the kids an assignment, I tell them exactly what I want, why we're doing the assignment, and how many points it's worth. They're trying harder now than they did before."

    _____

Chapter 10

Jan, a kindergarten teacher, Rod, a fifth grade teacher, an eighth grade physical science teacher named Dawn, and Joe, a 10th grade world history teacher are all at a party and begin talking "shop," specifically about how they manage their classrooms.
  Assume their students' characteristics are consistent with patterns identified by research.

1. The one for whom establishing explicit boundaries and predictable consequences is most critical is:
   a. Jan.
   b. Rod.
   c. Dawn.
   d. Joe.
2. The one whose students need rules to be explicitly taught, practiced and reinforced is:
   a. Jan.
   b. Rod.
   c. Dawn.
   d. Joe.

3. Students finish a worksheet in Mrs. Wood's class, while she is working with a reading group. When individuals are finished, they get up from their desks and deposit the worksheet in a folder at the front of the room. Mrs. Wood continues working with the reading group without saying anything to the students doing the worksheet. This process best illustrates which of the following?
   a. A classroom procedure
   b. A classroom rule
   c. Teacher withitness
   d. Teacher overlapping

4. As Mrs. Hayes is helping Janet with one of the problems on the seatwork assignment, Rene, who has had her hand up, nearly shouts, "Mrs. Hayes, I can't do this one. I've had my hand up for five minutes."
   "Please," Mrs. Hayes pleads looking over her shoulder. "Must you yell? I can't be in two places at once. Try and be patient, and I'll get there as soon as I can."
   Of the following, Mrs. Hayes behavior best illustrates which of the following?
   a. An "I-message"
   b. A passive response
   c. An assertive response

d. A hostile response

e. Active listening

5. Mrs. Vitale, an American History teacher, is discussing factors leading up to the War of 1812, such as the "impressment" of Americans into the British navy, and Jefferson's effort to deal with the problem. In the process she adds a discussion of Jefferson's personal wide range of interests including examples, and then turns back to her discussion of factors leading up to the war.

From the perspective of "lesson movement" as a classroom management factor which of the following is the best analysis?

a. Her presentation is inappropriate because adding the information about Jefferson's personal life would detract from lesson "smoothness."

b. Her presentation is appropriate because adding the information about Jefferson's personal life would be motivating.

c. Her presentation is inappropriate because she wouldn't be able to maintain "withitness" as she presents the information.

d. Her presentation would be inappropriate because some of the information is in the form of "dangles."

Read the case study involving Judy Holmquist and her 9th graders on page 93. Then answer items 6-12.

6. Look at 2-3 in Judy's lesson. Of the following, they best illustrate:

a. effective lesson communication.

b. effective lesson organization.

c. effective lesson overlapping.

d. ineffective teacher withitness.

7. Look at 7-12 in Judy's lesson. Of the following, these paragraphs best illustrate:

a. momentum and smoothness.

b. overdwelling and overlapping.

c. pacing and fragmentation.

d. withitness and overlapping.

e. dangles and flip-flops.

8. Look again at 7-12 in Judy's lesson. Of the following, Judy's behavior in the lesson best illustrates:

a. effective lesson organization.

b. effective communication.

c. effective lesson movement.

d. positive teacher characteristics.

9. In 7 Kevin taps Alison with his foot, and Judy intervenes in 8. She then moves to Sondra and asks her to move in 13. Judy's choosing to first deal with Kevin and then Sondra best illustrates which of the following:

a. withitness.

b. overlapping.

c. momentum.

d. smoothness.

e. fragmentation.

10. Look at 19 in Judy's lesson. Of the following this paragraph best illustrates:

a. positive teacher characteristics.

b. effective organization.

c. effective lesson movement.

d. effective communication.

11. Look at Judy's responses to Sondra in 15, 16, and 19. Of the following her responses best illustrate:

a. a passive response.

b. an assertive response.
  c. a hostile response.
12. Explain how Judy demonstrated each of the characteristics of teacher withitness in her lesson. Defend your explanation with information taken directly from the case study.

Chapter 10: Case Study for Practice Test Items

1. Judy Holmquist is a ninth-grade geography teacher whose class is involved in a cultural unit on the Middle East. She has 32 students in a room designed for 24, so the students are sitting within arm's reach across the aisles.
2. As Ginger comes in the door, she sees a large map projected high on the screen at the front of the room. She quickly slides into her seat just as the bell stops ringing. Most of the students have already begun studying the map and directions stating, *Identify the longitude and latitude of Cairo and Damascus.*
3. Judy takes roll and hands back a set of papers as the students busy themselves with the task. As she hands Brad his paper, she touches him on the arm and points to the overhead, reminding him to return from his window gazing.
4. She waits a moment for the students to finish and then pulls a large map down in the front of the classroom and begins a discussion with them.
5. "We've been studying the Middle East, and you just identified Damascus here in Syria," she notes pointing at the map. "Now, think for a moment and make a prediction about the climate in Damascus."
6. Judy pauses, surveys the class and says, "Kim?" as she walks down one of the rows.
7. ". . . Damascus is about 34 degrees north latitude, I think." As soon as Judy walks past him, Kevin sticks his foot across the aisle tapping Alison on the leg with his shoe, while he watches Judy's back from the corner of his eye. "Stop it Kevin," Alison mutters swiping at him with her hand.
8. Judy turns, steps back up the aisle and continues, "Good, Kim. It's very close to 34 degrees," and standing next to Kevin asks, "What would that indicate about its temperature at this time of the year? . . . Kevin?" she continues looking directly at him.
9. ". . . I'm not sure."
10. "Warmer or colder than here?"
11. ". . . Warmer, I think."
12. "OK, good prediction, Kevin, and why might that be the case? Jim?"
13. "Move up here," Judy directs quietly to Sondra, who has been whispering and passing notes to Sherrill across the aisle. Judy nods to a desk at the front of the room, as she waits for Jim to answer.
14. "What did I do?" Sondra protested.
15. Judy leans over Sondra's desk and points to a rule displayed on a poster saying,

Speak only when recognized by the teacher.

16. "Quickly, now," she motions to the desk.
17. ". . . Damascus is south of us and also in a desert," Jim responds.
18. "I wasn't 'speaking'," Sondra went on.
19. "Quickly now, Sondra. I have to interrupt my teaching when people aren't paying attention. I get worn out and frustrated when I'm interrupted. Please move," Judy said evenly, looking Sondra in the eye.
20. "Good analysis, Jim. Now, let's look at Cairo," she continues as she watches Sondra move to the new desk.

Chapter 11

1. Kevin Grimley has planned carefully for a lesson on the parts of flowering plants. In his plan is a detailed procedure that specifies each of the steps in the lesson. Jeanna Murphy has also planned carefully, but she hasn't written a procedure as detailed as Kevin's. If their behavior when they teach the lesson is consistent with patterns identified by research, which of the following is most likely?
    a. Kevin is more likely to change and adapt his instruction than is Jeanna, if the students indicate that they're confused.

b. Jeanna is more likely to change and adapt her instruction than is Kevin if the students indicate that they're confused.

c. There will be no significant difference in the extent to which the teachers change and adapt their instruction.

2. You're a physical education teacher. You want your students to think that health and fitness are important and should be a part of their lifestyle. Your goal would be best classified as:
   a. cognitive.
   b. affective.
   c. psychomotor.
   d. both cognitive and psychomotor.
   e. both affective and psychomotor.

3. Consider the objective: "In sentences embedded in a paragraph, students will identify the adjective clauses."

   Which of the following is the best assessment of the objective using Mager's criteria for acceptable objectives?
   a. OK as written.
   b. Missing or improperly stated condition.
   c. Missing or improperly stated behavior.
   d. Missing or improperly stated criterion.

4. Consider the objective: "Understands hyperbole; 1. Identifies statements of hyperbole in a paragraph with 100% accuracy."

   Which of the following is the best assessment of the objective using Gronlund's criteria for acceptable objectives?
   a. OK as written.
   b. Missing general goal.
   c. Improperly stated general goal.
   d. Improperly stated specific behavior.

5. You give your students drawings of a rectangle, circle, trapezoid, and parallelogram and you want them to find the volume of each. At which level of the cognitive taxonomy is this task best classified?
   a. Knowledge
   b. Comprehension
   c. Application
   d. Analysis
   e. Synthesis

Chapter 12

1. Mrs. Haimowitz enjoys teaching, and she particularly enjoys teaching literature. "Let's get Mrs. H. off on one of her tangents today," Jerry whispers to Tina as they come into her class.

   "No problem," Tina responds. "I'll ask her about her trip to Spain when she saw the running of the bulls in Pamplona. That should take most of the period."

   Of the following, the concept most closely related to the illustration is:
   a. academic focus.
   b. allocated time.
   c. enthusiasm.
   d. modeling.
   e. questioning.

2. Darcia Myers, an 8th grade English teacher, typically spends about 7 minutes after the bell rings taking role, handing out papers, and writing assignments on the board. Bonnie Ossi, who teaches in the room next to Darcia, writes her assignments on the board during the time the students are moving from one class to another. Based on this information, which of the following conclusions is most valid?
   a. Darcia's allocated time is greater than Bonnie's.
   b. Darcia's engaged time will be greater than Bonnie's
   c. Bonnie's allocated time is greater than Darcia's.
   d. Bonnie's instructional time will be greater than Darcia's.
   e. Bonnie's academic learning time will be greater than Darcia's.

3. Teachers commonly complain about interruptions from the intercom. These disruptions typically most directly impact:
   a. allocated time.
   b. instructional time.
   c. engaged time.
   d. academic learning time.

4. Ms. Jeffrey's says to her students, "Let's do this once more. What did Timmy just say about the setting of the story?"
      This question is most closely related to:
   a. emphasis.
   b. enthusiasm.
   c. closure.
   d. feedback.

5. Look again at Ms. Jeffrey's and her question (in Item 4). Of the following, the question most closely relates to:
   a. focus.
   b. organization.
   c. communication.
   d. review and closure.

6. You are studying direct objects with your students and you display the following sentence on the board.

   Ramon kicked the ball to Jack.

   You ask Alice, one of your students, "What is the direct object in the sentence?" Alice sits quietly, saying nothing. According to research, which of the following statements or questions is most effective?
   a. "Can someone help Alice out here?"
   b. "Look, Alice, the sentence says 'Ramon kicked the *ball*.' *Ball* is the direct object."
   c. "The direct object receives the action of the verb. *Ball* is the direct object."
   d. "What did Ramon kick, Alice?"

7. Two teachers were beginning a study of longitude and latitude with their 7th grade geography students. Mrs. Ramos began by telling the students that they met a new friend from another state. In asking the students how they might be able to tell their new friend where they lived, and the discussion that followed, she led them to the idea of longitude and latitude being a way to determine exact location, and she helped them identify longitude and latitude lines on the globe and find the locations of theirs and other cities using longitude and latitude.

Mr. Von Kleist showed the students a globe and told them that distances were measured using longitude and latitude. He carefully defined both and showed the students examples of the longitude and latitude of several locations on the globe and plane maps.

Which teacher's approach was more *constructivist*?

a. Mrs. Ramos's approach, because she her lesson began with a problem and the students' understanding was developed around a solution to the problem.

b. Mr. Von Kleist's, because he showed the students several examples of longitude and latitude on the globe.

c. Mrs. Ramos's, because she had the students find the location of the own city using longitude and latitude.

d. Mr. Ramos's, because he used both a globe and plane maps.

Read the case study describing Nicole Moseko's teaching on pages 97 and 98, and use it as a basis for answering the following questions, 8-15.

8. Of the following features of essential teaching skills, paragraph 6 best illustrates:
   a. modeling.
   b. sensory focus.
   c. monitoring.
   d. organization.

9. Look at paragraph 35. Of the following, this paragraph best illustrates:
   a. enthusiasm.
   b. modeling.
   c. emphasis.
   d. connected discourse.

10. Of the following features of essential teaching skills, paragraphs 46-56 best illustrate:
   a. organization.
   b. emphasis.
   c. focus.
   d. feedback.
   e. review and closure.

11. Think about Nicole's lesson as an application of the direct instruction model. Of the following, the step in the model that Nicole emphasized least was:
   a. introduction and review.
   b. presentation.
   c. guided practice.
   d. independent practice.

For items 12-14 look again at Nicole Moseko's lesson and identify the essential teaching skill and the particular element of the skill asked for in the item. (For example, for paragraph 42 you would respond "Attitudes—enthusiasm.")

12. Look at paragraph 4 in Nicole's lesson. The skill best illustrated in this paragraph is:

   _____

13. Look at 5. The skill best illustrated in this paragraph is:

   _____

14. Look at 13-17 in Nicole's lesson. The skill best illustrated in the combination of these paragraphs is:

   _____

15. Write an assessment of Nicole's questioning in her lesson. Defend your assessment with information taken directly from the case study.

Chapter 12: Case Study Involving Nicole Moseko and Her Students

1. Nicole Moseko, a second year teacher, was sitting at her desk after school, reading her notes as she planned for the next day. In a journal, she had written simple, short comments about her units and lessons as she taught them and so she could refer to them when she planned lessons for these topics the next time.

2. She reacted with a nod when she read, "Don't know the basic concepts—can't find areas," in a note referring to a section on finding the area of irregularly shaped plane figures. She was preparing for the same section and was planning carefully, because she knew the students would have a rough time. She smiled wryly when she remembered how frustrated she was when she taught the same section last year.

3. Nicole reflected on her experience and decided that she needed to be more thorough this year. "I'll review the basic concepts first," she thought to herself, "and then be sure they can find those areas," as she moved over to the computer in her room. She used it to quickly prepare three sheets, one with a series of basic figures on it and two others with a series of irregularly shaped figures. She then went down to the copy machine and made a transparency of each sheet.

4. "They're going to get it this year," she mumbled to herself with determination as she walked back to her room.

5. As the students walked into the class the next morning they glanced at the overhead to see what problem Nicole had given them for their "warm-up," she finished taking roll while they solved the problem, and she watched as they passed their papers forward.

6. She then began by displaying an overhead and saying, "OK everybody, let's take a moment to look at some drawings I've put together for our next section. What do you see here?" and Nicole then displayed a series of irregularly shaped polygons on the overhead.

7. The class observed that they were all funny shaped, and Nicole then went on, "Now, let's keep these figures in mind as we review, because we want to figure out how to find the area for each of them. This is what we're after for this section."

8. "Now," she continued, "take a look at this overhead," and she displayed a series of basic shapes—square, rectangle, triangle, rhombus, circle, parallelogram, trapezoid, sphere, cone, and cube.

9. "Let's identify each of the shapes," she went on. She reviewed the names of each shape with the class, and then said, "Now, look carefully. How are 8, 9, and 10 different from the others?" she asked pointing at the sphere, cone, and cube. "Kelly?"

10. ". . . They're not flat like the others."

11. "Exactly! Very good. They're solid figures, and in this section we're only dealing with plane figures. Which means what? Jan?"

12. ". . . What means what?" Jan responded, not understanding the question.

13. "What does *plane figure* mean?" Nicole rephrased.

14. ". . ."

15. "How many dimensions does it have?"

16. ". . . Two."

17. "Right, Jan! And how many dimensions does a solid have? Joe?"

18. "Three."

19. "All right. So, now away we go. We know that we're dealing with only plane figures for now. Let's look at the way we find the area for each."

20. The class looked at the formulas for finding the areas of the square, rectangle, triangle and circle. After reviewing the formula for each, she said, "Now, let's look. Let's compare the formulas for finding the area of a square, rectangle and parallelogram. Look at the square and rectangle first. Teri?"

21. ". . . I think they're actually the same."

22. "Good, Teri. And why do you say that?"

23. ". . . Well, it's actually length times width in both cases. Only with the square the length and width are the same, so it comes out length squared or width squared, whichever way you want to look at it."

24. "Excellent thinking, Teri! Now, let's look at the rectangle and parallelogram. How do you suppose we could figure out a formula for the area of the parallelogram."

25. In the course of the discussion, Nicole drew two lines in the parallelogram as shown in the drawing below, and led the students to the formula by using the formulas for the rectangle and the triangle.

26. "Look a little more closely at the two," Nicole continued. "What else to you notice about the rectangle and parallelogram?"

27. "..."
28. "Tell us the characteristics of the parallelogram again. Nikki?"
29. "The opposite sides are equal and parallel."
30. "Good. Now look at the rectangle."
31. "... Hey! I see," Brad interjected after studying the two. "A rectangle is really a parallelogram."
32. "What makes you say that?" Nicole smiled.
33. "The opposite sides *are* equal and parallel in the rectangle. It's just that the angles are all 90 degrees."
34. "Outstanding thinking. Did everyone see what Brad did? He compared similarities and differences between rectangles and parallelograms. This is exactly the kind of thinking we're after. We're trying to find the relationships among the different figures. That way we'll get the parts to fit together."
35. "Let's try it again. Look at the rhombus."
36. The class quickly identified the rhombus as another subset of parallelograms.
37. Nicole, obviously pleased, smiled and then went on, "Now suppose our parallelogram looked like this," and she drew a picture of a *trapezoid* on the chalkboard.
38. "How would we have to adapt our formula? Bruce?"
39. "We wouldn't have a parallelogram anymore."
40. "Good, Bruce, and why not? Kathy?"
41. "Only one set of sides are parallel," Kathy responded quickly, warming to the task. "It's a trapezoid."
42. "Hey, you people are getting good at this!" Nicole responded eagerly, as she thought to herself, "This is sure working better than last year."
43. The class then attacked the problem of finding the area of the trapezoid.
44. "Hey, let's make a rectangle and two triangles again!" Jim suggested.
45. The class derived a solution for finding the area of the trapezoid and compared it to both the rectangle and the parallelogram.
46. "Now what have we been doing here?" Nicole asked swooping her hand in an arc.
47. "..."
48. "What have we found in these shapes? ... Kind of a what? ... Kerry?"
49. "... We compared them," Kerry offered tentatively.
50. "Yes we did. Good! And in comparing them we found a ...? Steve?"
51. "... A pattern?" Steve responded hesitantly.
52. "Exactly! That's precisely what we did. Finding patterns is one of the most basic processes there is in thinking. Excellent, everyone."
53. Nicole then continued by asking, "Now, what was the point in all this? Anyone?"
54. "We were searching for patterns."
55. "Yes! Excellent! And what else did I tell you to keep in mind at the beginning of the period?"
56. "... We're going to do the same thing we did here to find the areas of the funny looking figures," Sue volunteered.
57. "Precisely!" Nicole waved. "That's where we'll begin tomorrow. To get us started, let's try a couple." She then handed the students the third sheet she had prepared, which had on it a series of irregular polygons.
58. "Let's look at the first one. Does anything in that figure look familiar? Jeremy?"
59. "The pointy part looks like a triangle," Jeremy replied.
60. "Good, and if we drew a line across here at the base of the triangle, what would we have below it? Kim."
61. "A square."
62. "Excellent, Kim. Does everybody see what we've done? We've taken the irregularly shaped polygon and broken it into sub parts—a triangle and a square. How many of you now think you can find the area of this polygon. ... Good, everyone thinks so. ... Now, for tomorrow do all three, and we'll see how we make out."
63. "Just to be sure we're comfortable with where we're headed, how are we going to attack the problems? Kevin?"
64. "... When we see an irregularly shaped polygon, we're first going to see if we can break it down into familiar shapes. Then we can find the area for each one and add up the areas."
65. "Outstanding everyone. Go to it. You should be able to get all three done by the end of the period. If you have any problems, raise your hands, and I'll come and help you. ... Get good at this, because we're going to have some challenging ones tomorrow."
66. The students then worked on the problems for the remainder of the period.

Chapter 13

You are conducting a question and answer activity to review the parts of the cell with your class of 27 students. In your review you call on about two-thirds of the students, and most of them answer the questions correctly. You conclude that the class understands the material.

1. Of the following, noticing that the students answer most of the questions correctly best illustrates:
   a. a formal measurement.
   b. an informal measurement.
   c. an evaluation.
   d. an assessment system.
2. Of the following, your conclusion best illustrates:
   a. a formal measurement.
   b. an informal measurement.
   c. an evaluation.
   d. an assessment system.
3. Which of the following best describes your conclusion?
   a. It is reliable but not valid.
   b. It is both reliable and valid.
   c. It is unreliable and therefore invalid.
   d. It is invalid and therefore unreliable.

4. Joe Williams and David Negge both have "the students' ability to make and defend an argument" as a goal for their students. They both assign an essay where the students have to take and defend a position as to whether or not Spain's, Britain's, and France's goal in exploring the New World in the 16th and 17th centuries was economic or not. Joe constructs a set of criteria to be used in scoring the essay. David does not. They both score the essays and assign students' grades. Of the following, which is the most accurate statement?
   a. David's assessment is likely to be less reliable than Joe's and therefore less valid as well.
   b. David's assessment is likely to be less reliable than Joe's but they are equally valid.
   c. Both teachers' assessments are likely to be invalid, since they are essays.
   d. Both teachers' assessments are valid and reliable since the assessments are consistent with their goals.

5. Jim Mittel is philosophically opposed to tests with his fourth graders on the grounds that it puts them in an anxiety laden situation. He assigns grades based on their responses in class, arguing, "I call on all the students regularly, and I can tell from their answers whether or not they understand the content." Based on this information, which of the following is the most accurate statement?
   a. His assessments are likely to be valid but not reliable.
   b. His assessments are likely to be reliable but not valid.
   c. His assessments are likely to be both valid and reliable.
   d. His assessments are likely to be both <u>invalid</u> and <u>unreliable</u>.

6. Kathy, one of Mrs. Mahoney's students in 10th grade honors English, got a high B the first grading period and an A– the second grading period. Mrs. Mahoney commented periodically on Kathy's good work on her essays. However, Kathy didn't score particularly highly on the PSAT, scoring in the 48th percentile on the verbal section. By comparison, most of the rest of the class scored in the 80th percentile or higher. The results were sent to Mrs. Mahoney, who then passed them along to Kathy.

   Kathy's father, proofread her essays as she had done the first two grading periods, but Kathy got a C the third grading period. "I'll bring it back up, Dad," she vowed. However, she got another C the fourth grading period and also got a C for the year.

Based on the information in the case study, which of the following is the most likely explanation for the decline in Kathy's grades?
   a. Her motivation declined, and with it, the quality of her work.
   b. Kathy's self-esteem was lowered as a result of her modest performance on the PSAT and as a result her performance suffered.
   c. Having scored lower than her peers, Kathy no longer felt capable of competing with them and her efforts were reduced.
   d. Mrs. Mahoney's perception of Kathy's ability was adversely affected by Kathy's PSAT results.

Use the following information for items 7 and 8.

Four teachers were discussing their test-anxious students.

Mrs. Rowe commented, "I have them practice on items that are exactly like those that will be on the test. Then I try to motivate them by mentioning in passing that some of the items on the test will challenge them, and they're going to have to do some thinking."

"I do the same thing, meaning I have them practice," Mr. Potter comments, "but I don't say anything one way or the other about how difficult the test will be."

"I do stress reduction activities with my class," Mrs. Richards adds. "Just before we begin the test, I have them close their eyes, visualize themselves doing well on the test, and take a few deep breaths. Then we start."

"I do something a little different, "Mr. Lareau adds. "I tell them that I know they will do well, and I tell them to be ready for a test every day, because I'm not going to tell them when we're having it, except that it will be sometime during the week. It keeps them on their toes."

7. Based on research, the teacher *most* effective in reducing test anxiety in her students is likely to be:
   a. Mrs. Rowe
   b. Mr. Potter
   c. Mrs. Richards
   d. Mr. Lareau
8. Based on research, the teacher *least* effective in reducing test anxiety in her students is likely to be:
   a. Mrs. Rowe
   b. Mr. Potter
   c. Mrs. Richards
   d. Mr. Lareau

Use the following information for items 9-10.

Gigi Parker is emphasizing grammatically correct writing and expression of thought in writing with her students. She has begun using *portfolios,* where systematic collections of her students' are placed for review and evaluation. She puts work samples in the portfolio at least three days a week, and she is careful to date the samples to help in assessing her students' progress. In examining her students' work, she checks for grammar, punctuation, spelling, and clear expression of thought, and she assigns grades on that basis.

9. If Gigi is consistent with patterns identified by research, which of the following is most likely?
   a. Gigi is an elementary teacher.
   b. Gigi is a middle school teacher.
   c. Gigi is a high school teacher.
10. Based on the information about Gigi's assessments, which of the following is the most accurate statement?
   a. They are likely to be both reliable and valid.
   b. They are likely to be reliable but not valid.

c. They are likely to be valid but not reliable.

d. They are likely to be both <u>in</u>valid and <u>un</u>reliable.

A subtest of a standardized test has a mean of 40 with a standard deviation of 4. (Assume a very large sample so the test results nearly fit a normal distribution.) George scores a 46 on the subtest.

11. Based on this information, the best approximation of the following of George's percentile rank is:

   a. 40
   b. 44
   c. 84
   d. 90
   e. 98

12. Cory scores a 44 on the same subtest. Of the following the best description of Cory's stanine is:

   a. 5
   b. 6
   c. 7
   d. 8
   e. 9

13. You have two sets of scores, which are as follows:

   Set A: Mean—40   Median—40   Standard deviation—4
   Set B: Mean—40   Median—41   Standard deviation—6

   Of the following, which is the most accurate statement?
   a. The students' performance for both sets was equal since the means are the same.
   b. The scores in Set B tend to be spread out more than the scores in Set A.
   c. The students in Set B actually performed better since the standard deviation is higher than in Set A.
   d. The students in Set B actually performed better since both the median and standard deviation are higher than they are in Set A.

14. Look at the following test item.

   Which of the following is a function of the digestive system?
   a. To circulate the blood.
   b. To protect vital body organs.
   * c. To digest the food we eat and turn it into usable fuel for our bodies.
   d. To transfer nerve impulses.

   There are at least three problems with this item. Identify the problems. Then rewrite the item to make it more acceptable.

PRACTICE TEST ITEMS
ANSWERS

Chapter 2

1. b Jimmy is centering on the large and small numbers and is ignoring the fact that the small one is on top and the larger one is on the bottom. He subtracts the smaller from the larger regardless of their position.
2. d Subtracting the smaller from the larger number allowed Jimmy to remain at equilibrium.
3. a The soccer ball is the most concrete example. Also, there would be no point in showing a picture of a girl when the class has several real girls in it.
4. d When learners are unable to understand information, assuming they have the ability, lack of experience is usually the cause.
5. b The model is the only one that illustrates the process. Melting the ice merely illustrates change of state and doesn't illustrate anything about the motion of the molecules.
6. c Assimilation and accommodation are types of adaptation.
7. b Jackie is classifying on the basis of a perceptual feature, which is characteristic of preoperations.
8. d
9. b According to Kathy, Ron doubts himself.
10. d Ron "knows what kind of a guy" he is.
11. c Students at this age are attempting to establish an identity.
12. d Cliff is demonstrating the characteristics of integrity.
13. b This demonstrates reciprocity.
14. b Joey is demonstrating stage 3 morality. This requires concrete operations, which means he can be no younger than 9.
15. Stage 1
16. Stage 3
17. Stage 3
18. Stage 4
19. Stage 5
20. Stage 4

Chapter 3

1. a The fact that she used *concrete materials* was the key factor in the effectiveness of her teaching.
2. d The concept of volume is more abstract than the concept of cube. The students have to think logically to attain the concept of volume, while the concept of cube is essentially perceptual.
3. d While first graders are at a point where they're making the transition to concrete operations, they're likely to make their conclusions based on perception.
4. a Mr. Johnson provided the necessary experience to help the students understand the concepts, and the students can see the four squares in each case. Because the students are *chronologically* concrete operational doesn't mean they will be able to perform the task if they haven't had the prerequisite experience (choice b).
5. a The sequence illustrated in choice a begins with the most concrete experiences and ideas first and then proceeds to the more abstract ideas. None of the other three sequences follows this pattern.
6. b Mrs. Grimley used a combination of modeling and positive reinforcement to help her students understand the need to pay attention.

7. d Mrs. Patterson used modeling and reinforcement to encourage her students in their efforts to pay attention. Her use of modeling wasn't as explicit and direct as Mrs. Lamb's and therefore was slightly less effective. (David served as the model.)

8. c Mr. Minchew didn't actually teach his students what paying attention means, and second graders may not understand the concept of attention merely from stating it in a rule. Further, he used punishment when they were inattentive rather than reinforcing attentive behaviors.

9. d Research indicates that students need to feel a sense of accomplishment in their work in order to have high academic self-esteem. (See pages 117-119 of your text for a discussion of this topic.)

10. c Research indicates that early-maturing boys are often more poised, popular and self-assured than their later-maturing counterparts, while early-maturing girls tend to be more introverted and shy.

11. a The negative effects of early and late maturation are generally mild for most youngsters.

12. a Girls' verbal ability at this age tends to be more advanced than does boys'.

Chapter 4

1. a Intelligence tests measure experience, and Sandi's experience is limited.

2. c Sandi picks up ideas rapidly and tends to think more in the abstract than do her peers.

3. a Her mother is a high school dropout with a low status, low paying job.

4. d Students from low SES backgrounds are about twice as likely to drop out as are students from the general population.

5. b Gardner identifies interpersonal skills as one of the seven dimensions of intelligence.

6. c Research indicates that the mix of students and teachers' expectations for students exert a powerful effect on their achievement.

7. c Being placed in low-ability classes tends to stigmatize students which results in lowered self-concepts and poorer attitudes toward learning.

8. a Based on Ogbu's work, Henry best fits the description of an *involuntary* minority, and therefore, is most likely to experience *cultural inversion.*

9. d Treating students equally is important. All should be included. Open-ended questions are an excellent tool for working with all students.

10. c According to research patterns, teachers tend to address higher level questions to boys than they do to girls.

11. a According to research, teachers also tend to direct more questions to boys than to girls.

12. Gabriella has several characteristics of at-risk students. She is a low SES, cultural minority, whose native language is not English. Her mother is divorced. However, Gabriella appears to be an intelligent girl. Her teacher needs to "keep an eye on her." It is important for her teacher to make her feel wanted and included in the school environment.

Chapter 5

1. a Due process through parental involvement guarantees parents access to their student's records.

2. d The law requires that tests be given in a student's native language. The other three choices are within the law.

3. c The law requires that no single instrument be used as the sole basis for placement in a special education program.

4. a The law does speak to the offer of an independent evaluator, saying that the offer should be made.

5. d The law requires parents' signatures on IEPs.

6. a Teachers tend to confuse being a model student with being gifted, and minorities tend to be underrepresented in programs for the gifted.

7. a Any students who have characteristics that can keep them from reaching their maximum potential in the regular classroom are classified as having an exceptionality.
8. e Boys are from three to nine times more likely than girls to be diagnosed as having ADD-H

Chapter 6

1. b Mr. Soo's positive manner becomes associated with Tim's mother. Mr. Soo jokes with Tim *in his mother's presence.* (Tim's mother is the unconditioned stimulus, and the happiness Tim feels when with her is the unconditioned response.)
2. d Since Mr. Soo remains, and he has become associated with Tim's mother, he elicits the conditioned response—satisfaction. Happiness—the unconditioned response—and satisfaction are similar emotions.
3. a The school has become associated with Mrs. Hafner's warmth. (Mrs. Hafner's warmth is an unconditioned stimulus which resulted in the unconditioned response—relief. Since Martina's father merely drops her off, neither Mrs. Hafner nor the school have become associated with him, so he is not the unconditioned stimulus.)
4. d Martina feels at-ease when she enters the school, so this feeling is the conditioned response.
5. a There is not evidence in the example about successive approximations to a more complete or fully developed behavior, so shaping isn't occurring.
6. c His behavior is being reduced, so it is punishment. The students are *presenting* him with their complaints. (The behavior is voluntary, so it is not a conditioned response.)
7. b An undesirable situation—the length and difficulty of the test—is being reduced, so the students' complaints are being negatively reinforced. (Their complaints occur sooner, so their complaining behavior is increasing.)
8. e Jamey's verbal behavior is saying, "Give." This behavior is increasing, so it is reinforcement.
9. b Her encouragement is a form of reinforcement, and "every few minutes" is a variable interval.
10. c Mrs. Batton's comment is a positive reinforcer for Jimmy.
11. d The other students are being vicariously reinforced by Mrs. Batton's compliment directed to Jimmy.
12. d Jimmy is serving as a model for the other students.
13. d Mrs. Locke is requiring Li to give more complete responses in order to be reinforced.
14. d Even though Mrs. Massey gives a quiz every day, not all "studying" behaviors are reinforced; for example, students will study at night, but they are not reinforced until they perform on the quizzes. Each day is predictable, as is a Tuesday/Thursday schedule, so both are fixed interval.
15. a) Since Jimmy's behavior is increasing—he says, "I don't know," sooner the second time than he did the first time—he is being reinforced. The reinforcer is Mr. Hanson "removing" the question from him (taking him off the "hook"), so it is an example of negative reinforcement. b) Jimmy is likely to say, "I don't know," even sooner than he did before. c) Mr. Hanson should give Jimmy some prompts or cues that will allow him to answer instead of turning the question to another student.

Chapter 7

1. a These teacher behaviors attract attention.
2. b When students respond to open-ended questions, they describe what the stimulus means to them, which indicates their perception.
3. a Practice puts the students in an active role, which aids encoding into long-term memory.
4. d Ben is attempting to elaborate on the features of parabolas to make ellipses more meaningful.
5. d The definition provides a link for the examples and vice versa, so meaningfulness is increased.

6. a   Information processing begins with attention, so we must first get the students' attention. Of the choices given, throwing a ball to a student is most likely to attract the students' attention.
7. a   Perception appears next to attention in the information processing model. Asking students questions to check their understanding of your examples is a form of checking perception. (Also, if the students rehearse misperceived information, invalid schemata will be formed in long-term memory.)
8. b   A chart, such as Luis's matrix is a way of *organizing* information.
9. c   The students' working memories were overloaded, so they lost some of the information. There is no evidence of rehearsal or misperception in the example.
10. d   Working exercises puts the students in an active role, which aids encoding.
11. d   Giselle is demonstrating both understanding of and control over her memory.
12. W,L
13. S,L
14. W,L
15. W (Automaticity describes information that takes up virtually no working-memory space, and for this reason, it most closely relates to working memory.)

Chapter 8

1. b   *Adverb* is a category with common characteristics.
2. d   The definition is a form of declarative knowledge. Many definitions are memorized until they are made more meaningful with the use of examples.
3. e   Names and labels are forms of declarative knowledge.
4. a   Names are typically memorized. They can sometimes be made more meaningful with the use of mnemonics.
5. e   The students were able to identify an example of a concept, and they were also able to describe what they had identified in words.
6. c   Ken is recognizing a rule. The adjective before the noun is arbitrary. For example in French it is just the opposite; the adjective follows the noun.
7. d   The sentence illustrates that the adjective describes the noun in each case; it provides context. The word *big* exists in isolation, so it doesn't illustrate the characteristics of *adjective*. The statement in choice *c* is merely declarative knowledge. The picture merely illustrates a large and small building. It doesn't illustrate the concept.
8. d   "Objects expand when they're heated" is a principle.
9. c   Putting the balloons in the hot water and ice respectively is the only choice that actually *illustrates* the relationship between heat and expansion.
10. b   Joanne is the most active in her choice of items to highlight. She makes a decision about what she thinks is important, and she highlights only that information.
11. c   Of the three students Brad is the least active. In his highlighting of complete passages he is involved in very little decision making about what is important and what isn't.
12. b   Mrs. D'Armas provided context by using the sentences and she had an example of an adverb modifying a verb, adjective, and another adverb. Mrs. Voltaire didn't have an example illustrating an adverb modifying another adverb.
13. a   Mrs. Evans provided no context for the examples.
14. Ideally the examples would be embedded in context, such as in the following passage:

Brooksville, a city in Ohio, has three high schools. As <u>Brooksville's</u> and other <u>cities'</u> schools strive for excellence, their programs continually improve.

The <u>city's</u> best school, Central High, has had a number of significant accomplishments. Four of <u>Central High's</u> girls earned high scholastic and athletic honors and the <u>girls'</u> honors reflect positively on everyone. One <u>girl's</u> long jump went over 16 feet, a new state record in that class. The <u>boys'</u> teams did equally well. One <u>boy's</u> English essay earned him a trip to New York City to participate in a young <u>writer's</u> contest.

Children's efforts in the elementary schools are equally noteworthy. Many of the children have written original short stories that have appeared as features in the local newspaper.

In all, the school system in Brooksville is one that makes everyone proud to be a resident. A rationale for the passage could be as follows:

> The passage provides context for the examples. The quality is quite good, since the students can determine both that the nouns are either singular or plural and whether or not they are possessive based on the passage. There are five examples of singular possessive nouns and four examples of plural possessive nouns, so the variety is also quite good.

Chapter 9

1. C   The suggestion that people are motivated by a need to "understand" is consistent with cognitive views of motivation.
2. A   The need to be "in with the guys" relates to a belonging need from Maslow's work, which is a humanistic orientation.
3. B   The person in this case is responding to the grade, which is external. It is a reinforcer for trying hard.
4. B   As with item 3, attention is external and is a reinforcer for the Steve.
5. S   The teacher in this case is trying to capitalize on both the *value* and the *success* component of expectancy × value theory.
6. C   Starting lessons with something unexpected is directed at students' need to "understand."
7. c   The information we have about Janet suggests that she is at the level of aesthetic appreciation, which, according to Maslow, implies that the deficiency needs are met. Growth needs are never "met," so we can't say that she is self-actualized nor can we say that her intellectual achievement need has been satisfied.
8. c   Jeff attributes his grade to luck, which is external.
9. a   At the extreme attributing lack of success to ability leads to a feeling of "what's the use in trying" which is learned helplessness.
10. d   People who link performance to effort are likely to have an incremental view of ability. While Billy attributed lack of success to lack of effort, he could be attempting to protect his self-worth by not trying. This is characteristic of people with an entity view of ability.
11. b   Billy not trying is an attempt to "look smart." Had he succeeded, he could conclude that he had high ability, since he was able to succeed without effort.
12. d   Linking achievement to effort is the most desirable attribution.
13. e   The best indicator of warmth and caring that exists is the willingness to spend time with learners.
14. Modeling
15. Success
16. Comprehension

Chapter 10

1. c   Boundaries and predictable consequences are most important for middle and junior high school students.
2. a   Young children need specifically taught, practiced, and reinforced rules and procedures.
3. a   Students depositing papers indicates that they understand a procedure.
4. b   Mrs. Hayes "pleading" and responding with indirect nonverbal behavior are indicators of a passive response.
5. a   Mrs. Vitale "flips-flops" in her discussion of factors leading up to the War of 1812, Jefferson's personal characteristics and back to the causes of the war. Flip-flops detract from lesson smoothness.

6. b The paragraphs indicate that the students were following a routine, which is part of effective lesson organization.

7. d In 7-12 Judy intervenes and stops Kevin's misbehavior while maintaining the flow of the lesson.

8. c Withitness and overlapping are part of lesson movement.

9. a Judy first intervened with Kevin because poking Alison with his foot was a more severe infraction than passing a note.

10. d Judy is using an "I-message," which according to Gordon is a form of effective communication.

11. b Judy was neither passive nor hostile. She communicated clearly in a no-nonsense way that Sondra was to move.

12. She intervened immediately (Kevin tapped Alison in 7, and she intervened in 8 by moving to him and calling on him); she caught the "right one" (she intervened with Kevin instead of Alison); and she dealt with the worst infraction first (she first dealt with Kevin and then Sondra).

Chapter 11

1. b Research indicates that when teachers write detailed procedures, they tend to follow the plan even if it isn't working.

2. b Though you're a PE teacher, wanting your students to think that "health and fitness are important" focuses on attitude, which is in the affective domain.

3. d The objective doesn't provide a criterion for acceptable performance.

4. d Gronlund specifically suggests that an objective should not contain criteria, such as "with 100% accuracy."

5. c The students need to both select the correct formula for solving the problems in each case, and then they must solve the problems. These are application level tasks.

Chapter 12

1. a When Mrs. H. gets off on her stories she loses academic focus. Losing focus has no impact on her allocated time (b), and though she likes teaching, we have no evidence about her enthusiasm (c), her modeling (d), or questioning (e).

2. d Darcia loses 7 minutes of instructional time with her administrative activities. Their allocated times are the same (a & c), we have no evidence to indicate Bonnie's engaged time will be greater than Darcia's (b), and we don't have evidence one way or the other about student success (e)

3. b Interruptions have no effect on allocated time (a), and we don't know about the extent to which they impact student success (d). They indirectly affect engaged time (c), but their most direct effect is on instructional time.

4. a "Let's do this once more . . ." illustrates repetition, which is a form of emphasis. We have no evidence one way or the other that the lesson is coming to a close.

5. c Ms. Jeffrey's is demonstrating emphasis, and emphasis is a part of communication.

6. d This is a prompting question, which keeps Alice actively involved in the process and will lead to a successful response. Choice a is least effective. Choices b and c give Alice feedback, but she is less active than she would be if you prompt her.

7. a A *constructivist* approach to instruction helps students develop their own understanding of topics. Instructional activities that exist in the form of problems to solve with understanding developed around the solution to those problems is characteristic of instruction based on constructivism.

8. b Nicole's display on the overhead is something for the students to look at.

9. c "Let's do it again" is a form of repetition, which is a type of emphasis.

10. e In these paragraphs Nicole is bringing the lesson to a close.

11. c   Nicole discusses with the students what they are supposed to do, but she does not actually conduct guided practice with them.
12. Attitude—expectations
13. Organization—established routines
14. Questioning—prompting
15. Nicole's questioning was effective according to research findings. She asked open-ended questions (e.g., "What do you see?" [6] and "How are they different?" [9]); she called on a wide variety of students (e.g., Kelly [9], Jan [11], Nikki [28], Bruce [38], Kathy [40], Kerry [48], Steve [50], Jeremy [58]); she prompted when a student was unable to answer (e.g., Jan [11-16]); and she promoted thinking with the kinds of questions she asked (e.g., "Why?" [22] and "What makes you say that?" [32]).

Chapter 13

1. b   Since you haven't gotten the same kind of information from each of the students, your observations are informal measurements.
2. c   Conclusions are evaluations.
3. c   Since different students answered different questions, and some students gave no answers at all, you haven't gotten reliable information. Unreliable information cannot be valid.
4. a   An unreliable assessment cannot be valid. Essays don't have to be invalid (choice c). In fact many goals can only be measured with essays. Choice d only refers to validity and doesn't address reliability.
5. d   His assessment cannot be reliable since different students are being asked different questions. Because his assessments are unreliable they cannot be valid.
6. d   We have no evidence to indicate that Kathy's motivation or self-esteem declined, and we do have evidence that she maintained her efforts. Also, teachers' expectations for their students strongly affect their assessments.
7. b   Giving students a chance to practice on items similar to those that will be on the text reduces anxiety. However, perception of difficulty increases anxiety (choice a).
8. d   Unannounced tests have a particularly adverse effect on test anxiety.
9. a   Elementary teachers use alternative assessments more than do middle or secondary teachers.
10. a   Her assessments are consistent with her goals, which promotes validity, and she is getting systematic information from all her students, which increases reliability.
11. d   George's score of 46 places him 1.5 standard deviations above the mean. In a normal distribution this places him at approximately the 90th percentile.
12. c   Cory's score of 44 places her one standard deviation above the mean. This falls in stanine 7.
13. b   The standard deviation doesn't imply better performance (choice c), nor does a combination of median and standard deviation (choice d). Based on equal means alone, we cannot conclude that the two groups performed equally (choice a).
14. The following are problems with the item.

1) The word *digest* is in the correct answer, which is closely related to the word digestive.
2) The correct answer is placed at choice "c".
3) The correct answer is significantly longer than the distracters.

The following would be one way to rewrite the item.

Which of the following is a function of the digestive system?
   a. To help move our blood throughout our bodies
   b. To protect our brain, heart, lungs, and other vital body organs
   c. To transfer nerve impulses from our brain to our muscles
 * d. To turn the food we eat into fuel for our bodies

Part IV
Observing in Classrooms: Exercises and Activities

In this, the fourth part of the supplement to your text, you will find a series of exercises that are designed to help you connect the content of the text to actual teaching practice. The exercises include suggestions for observing teachers as they work with their students, observing students in the learning activities, and for conducting interviews with teachers and students. The guidelines will help you get the most out of your time spent in schools.

As you spend time in schools, remember that you are a guest in another person's classroom. As a professional courtesy to the teachers, please keep the following points in mind.

1) Try to be unobtrusive. To the extent that you can, avoid interrupting classroom routines. It is a simple courtesy, and the information you gather will be more accurate if you aren't noticed.

2) Maintain the confidentiality of the teachers and students you observe. In any reports you make, avoid using last names and don't identify specific persons. You want to prevent the even remote possibility of embarrassing someone.

3) Keep the information you gather as factual as possible, and avoid making premature judgments. The purpose of your observations is to see the content of your text applied in classrooms; it is not to assess the teacher's performance. While you will certainly have some reactions to what the teacher does, try to report your observations as objectively as possible.

We turn now to specific suggestions and guidelines for each chapter. Good luck with your time spent in schools.

Chapter 1: Teaching in the Real World

Reflection
Teacher Interview: The first exercise focuses on teachers as reflective practitioners. To begin the interview you may want to provide a brief overview of the topic of reflection (See text pages 17-19). The following are some suggested questions:
1. When do you find opportunities to reflect about your teaching?
2. Can you give me a specific where you were involved in reflection in the last day or two?
3. Can you give me an example of how the process of reflection changed your teaching?
4. How do the following stimulate your thinking about teaching?
   - Interactions with students
   - Evaluations of student work
   - Interactions with parents or guardians
   - Conversations with other professionals
   - Research?
5. What changes in your professional life would give you greater opportunities to reflect?

Diversity
Student Observation: The purpose of this exercise is to gather basic information about the diversity found in the classroom. Seat yourself at the side of a room so that you can observe students during a lesson and as they enter and leave the room. Gather the following information:
1. Describe the students' sizes. How much do they differ in size? Who is the largest? Smallest?
2. How many males and females are there? How do they interact with each other?
3. Notice the students' clothes. Do they dress alike or is there considerable variation? Are the clothes new or do they appear well worn? Are they clean and in good repair? What do their shoes tell you?
4. How many different cultures appear to be represented? How can you tell? To what extent do students from different culture interact?

Teacher Interview: Explain to the teacher that the purpose of the interview is to gather information about diversity in classrooms. The following are some suggested questions.

1. How much do your students differ in ability?
2. What is the socioeconomic status of most students in your class? What is the range? How does this influence your teaching?
3. How many different cultures are represented in your classroom? For what percentage is English their first language? Is English spoken in the home? How does culture and language influence your teaching?
4. Do the boys and girls in your class do equally well in all subjects? Do they participate equally? Does student gender influence your teaching? If so, how?

Chapter 2: Student Development

Cognitive Development

Student Interview: The purpose of this exercise is to provide you with some experiences in conducting Piagetian tasks with students. If possible, conduct the interviews with a 5-6 year old, a 9-10 year old, and a 13-14 year old and compare their responses. If this isn't possible, interview several students at one grade level and compare their responses.

1. Conservation of Mass: Give the student two equal balls of clay. After the student confirms that they are equal, flatten one of the balls into a pancake shape. Ask:
   - Are the amounts of clay in the two pieces the same or different? How do you know?
2. Conservation of Volume: Show the student two identical clear containers partially filled with water. Ask if the amounts are the same. Then pour the water from one of the containers into a larger clear container. Ask:
   - Are the amounts of liquids in the two containers same or different? How do you know?
3. Conservation of Number: Arrange ten coins in two rows as they appear on page 46 of the text. Ask if the number of coins in the two rows is the same. Then rearrange them so the lower row is spread out. Ask:
   - Are the number of coins in the two rows the same or different? How do you know?
4. Control of Variables. Present the following problem to the student: I have ten puppies and I want to find out which of two kinds of dog food will make the puppies grow faster.
   - What kind of experiment could I do to answer the question?
   - Is there anything else I need to do?

Moral Development

Student Interview: As with the previous exercise try to select several students at different age levels to interview. If this is not possible, interview several students at the same level and pose these hypothetical dilemmas:

1. Cheating. This dilemma appears on page 63 of the text. You may want to simplify it if using it with younger students

   Steve, a high school junior, is working at a night job to help support his mother, a single parent of three. Steve is a conscientious student who works hard in his classes, but he doesn't have enough time to study. History isn't Steve's favorite course, and with his night work, he has a marginal <u>D</u> average. If he fails the final exam, he will fail the course, won't receive credit, and will have to alter plans for working during his senior year. He arranged to be off work the night before the exam so he could study extra hard, but early in the evening his boss called, desperate to have Steve come in and replace another employee who called in ill at the last moment. His boss pressured him heavily, so reluctantly Steve went to work at 8:00 p.m. and came home exhausted at 2:00 a.m. He tried to study, but fell asleep on the couch with his book in his lap. His mother woke him for school at 6:30.

   Steve went to his history class, looked at the test, and went blank. Everything seemed like a jumble. However, Jill, one of the best students in the class, happened to have her answer sheet positioned so he could clearly see every answer by barely moving his eyes.

- Is it OK for Steve to cheat? Why do you think so?
- What information in the story influenced your decision?
- Is it ever alright to cheat? If yes, when and why? If not, why not?

2. Honesty: Share the following situation with the student.

Kenny is walking to the store. It's his mother's birthday on Saturday. He's feeling bad because he hasn't been able to save up enough money to get her the present he'd like to give her. Then, on the sidewalk he finds a wallet with $10 in it—just what he needs to buy the present; but there's an identification card in the wallet telling the name and address of the owner.

- What should Kenny do? Why?
- What information in the story influenced your decision?
- Is it ever alright to keep something that doesn't belong to you? If yes, when and why? If not, why not?

Accommodating Developmental Diversity

Teacher Interview: Interview a teacher to determine how developmental diversity influences teaching. The following are some suggested questions:
1. How do the age and developmental level of your students influence your teaching? Can you give me specific examples?
2. How has your view of students changed as a result of working with them over time?
3. To what extent do you use the following strategies to accommodate diversity:
   - Design classroom experiences to specifically address background differences
   - Use concrete examples to illustrate abstract ideas
   - Use classroom interaction to encourage students to share their diverse experiences?

Chapter 3: Student Development: Applications

Students: Individual Differences

Student Observation: The purpose of this exercise is to begin exploring the developmental differences found in students. Ideally, it should be done in at least two different classes or at two different grade levels. Observe students and describe the following:
Physical Differences:
1. Describe the physical differences in the students.
2. Do these differences seem to have any effect on the way the students interact with each other or the way they behave in class? If they do, explain, including specific examples.
Energy and Attention Span:
1. How capable are students of monitoring their own attention spans?
2. How much do they fidget, play, and doodle during class?
3. How often does the teacher have to remind students to attend? Is it the group as a whole or certain students?
Gender Differences:
1. Do boys and girls participate equally? If not, who participates more? Is this in all classes or just certain ones?
2. Who do students sit next to? Talk to? Play with?
3. Are there differences in terms of behavioral problems?

Students' Language Differences

Teacher Interview: The purpose of this exercise is to examine language development and its effect on classroom performance. Interview a teacher. The following are some suggested questions:
1. Do all students speak English fluently?
2. Describe the differences in your students' language development.
3. What do you do to accommodate those differences?

4. Are there any English dialects spoken in your classroom? Do these dialects have any effect on classroom performance, such as in oral reports? Do they have any effect on the way the students interact with each other? Can you describe the effects?
5. Do you do anything to work with the dialects? If so, what?

Student Interview: Ask the teacher to help you identify several students who differ in their verbal skills. The following are some suggested questions:
1. Do you like school? What's the best part? The worst part?
2. Do you have many friends at school? Who are they? What do you do with them? Do your friends like school?
3. What is your favorite subject? Why do you like it? What is the hardest subject? What makes it hard?
4. If you could change one thing about school, what would it be? Why?

English as a Second Language

Teacher Interview: The following are some suggested questions for gathering information about students who are not native English speakers.
1. How many students are there with English as a second language? What countries do they come from?
2. How are the students' performing? Can you give some specific examples?
3. What programs exist for these students? How successful are they?
4. What do you do in the classroom to accommodate these language differences?

Student Observation: (Select several of these students and observe them during classroom instruction.) Try and answer the following questions:
1. How much do they participate in class? Do they volunteer?
2. Who do they talk to in class? Out of class? Who are their friends?
3. What special help are they given in the classroom? From the teacher? Other students? Special material? Pullout programs?

Chapter 4: Individual Differences

Ability Differences

Teacher Interview: Interview a teacher to gather information about the differences in student ability. The following are some suggested questions:
1. How much does the ability of your students vary?
2. What kind of information do you gather to help you deal with ability differences?
3. How do you group your students to deal with ability differences? How does it work?
4. What other strategies do you use to deal with ability differences?

Student Observation: Ask the teacher to identify two high and two low-ability students to observe. As you observe them describe the following:
1. How the two pairs of students differ in their ability to pay attention and stay on task?
2. Compare the participation of the two pairs. Specifically count the number of times students:
   - raise their hands to participate
   - are called on
   - answer questions correctly
   - are given positive feedback about their answers.
3. How the two pairs of students differ in terms of behavior problems?

Student Interview: If possible interview the students and ask:
1. How much do you like school?
2. What is your favorite part of school?
3. What is your best subject?
4. What is you hardest subject?

Socioeconomic Status

Teacher Interview: This exercise involves interviewing a teacher to examine how SES influences learning. The following are some suggested questions:
1. Describe the socioeconomic status of your students? How much do they vary?
2. How many of your students qualify for free or reduced-cost meals?
3. How many of your students come from single-parent families?
4. Do the parents support their children's efforts? Are they supportive of the school?
5. What do you do to accommodate the differences in SES among your students?

Culture

Teacher Interview: Interview a teacher and observe a classroom to examine how culture affects learning. The following are some suggested questions:
1. How many cultures are represented in your classroom? How many of your students belong to these different cultures?
2. How does culture affect learning in your classroom? Can you give me specific examples?
3. What modifications have you made in your teaching to accommodate cultural differences? How successful have they been? Can you give some specific examples?
4. What suggestions do you have for a beginning teacher working with students from different cultures?

Student Observation: Ask the teacher to provide you with a seating chart and identify students from different cultures. Observe the students and ask yourself the following:
1. Where do these students sit? (Is it by choice or assigned?)
2. Who do these students interact with?
3. How does the participation of these students compare to the participation of non-minorities?
4. How does their behavior (in terms of classroom management) compare to other students?

Learning Styles

Teacher Interview: Interview a teacher about his or students' learning styles. The following are some suggested questions:
1. Do your students have different learning styles (i.e., preferred ways of learning)? How can you tell?
2. Do you use any type of formal instrument to measure learning styles? Would you recommend it to others?
3. How do you modify your teaching to adjust to the learning styles of your students?

Chapter 5: Teaching Students with Exceptionalities

Public Law 94-142

Teacher Interview: Interview a teacher to discover how different components of Public Law 94-142 are implemented in the classroom. The following are some suggested questions:

Due Process Through Parental Involvement:
1. How are parents involved in the process?
2. What obstacles exist for greater parent involvement?
3. How are language barriers dealt with?

Protection Against Discrimination in Testing:
1. What provisions are made for ESL students?
2. How are classroom performance and general adaptive behavior assessed?

Least Restrictive Environment:
1. How does the concept of least restrictive environment work in your school?
2. Besides mainstreaming, what other options exist?

Individualized Education Program (IEP):
1. What does an IEP look like?

2. From your perspective what are the most important parts of the program? How well do they work? How could they be improved?

Mildly Handicapped Students

Teacher Interview: This exercise is intended to give you some information about a student having an exceptionality. Talk with a teacher to gather background experience about the student. The following are some suggested questions:

1. What kind of learning problem does the student have?
2. How did you discover this problem?
3. What help did you have in diagnosing the problem?
4. How do you use the IEP (ask to see it) to adapt instruction to the needs of the student?
5. What kinds of approaches (e.g., strategy, instruction, computer, social skills training) are being used to help the student?
6. Is supplementary instruction integrated or pull out?
7. How well is the student integrated into the regular flow of the classroom?
8. How well is the student accepted by other students?

Students with Physical Impairments

Teacher Interview: Work with the regular classroom teacher to identify a student with a physical impairment. Interview the teacher. The following are some suggested questions:

1. What kind of physical impairment is it?
2. How was it identified?
3. How does it affect the student's classroom performance?
4. How is instruction being adapted for the student?
5. How well is the student integrated into the regular flow of the classroom?
6. How well is the student accepted by other students?

Students Who Are Gifted and Talented

Teacher Interview: Interview a teacher and observe a program for gifted and talented students. The following are some suggested questions:

1. How are gifted and talented students defined?
2. How are these students identified?
3. What percentage of the student population is identified as gifted and talented?
4. Does the program emphasize enrichment or acceleration (see Table 5.7 in the text):
5. How well are gifted and talented students accepted and integrated into the regular classroom?

Chapter 6: Behavioral Views of Learning

Classical Conditioning: Classroom Climate

Classroom Observation: Observe in a classroom to investigate how the physical and social environment interact to create classroom climate. Ask yourself the following questions:
Physical Environment:

1. What kinds of things are on the wall (e.g., pictures, charts, diagrams)? Are there any plants? Does the room look like an inviting place to be?
2. What student work is displayed? (e.g., art work, projects, etc.)?
3. How are the desks arranged? What does this tell you about instruction?
4. Are there areas where students can go when their work is finished?
5. Are rules and procedures posted on the walls? Are these stated in a positive way?

Social Climate:

1. How do students enter the room? Do they seem glad to be there?
2. Do classes start in a positive, inviting way?
3. How does the teacher relate to students?
4. Is interaction in the classroom relaxed and easy?

Operant Conditioning

Classroom Observation: Observe a classroom and describe how the following are used:
Reinforcers:
1. Verbal reinforcers (e.g., praise, positive comments)
2. Tangible reinforcers (e.g., candy, pencils, etc.)
3. Token reinforcers (smiling faces, tickets, etc.)
4. Activity reinforcers (e.g., extra recess, time to work on the computer)

Punishment:
1. Verbal reprimands (e.g., "Mary, be quiet," "Jared, turn around")
2. Non-verbal reprimands (e.g., stern look, hand to lips)
3. Time out (e.g., isolation in corner of room or hall)
4. Lost privileges (e.g., Decreased recess, lunch time).
5. Call to parents
6. Visit to principal's office

Reinforcement Schedules

Classroom Observation: Observe a classroom and describe how different reinforcement schedules are implemented in the following areas:
Verbal Interaction:
1. Are correct responses reinforced every time? If not, how often are they reinforced?
2. How are incorrect, incomplete, or no responses reacted to?

Homework:
1. How often is homework given and collected?
2. Is homework graded every time, periodically, or sporadically? Do students know when it will be collected and graded?

Tests and Quizzes:
1. Are tests and quizzes announced beforehand?
2. Are tests and quizzes given on a regular basis? Is it determined by time or work (units) completed?

Observational Learning

Classroom Observation: Talk to a teacher and find out when they'll be using modeling to teach some concept or skill. Observe the lesson in terms of the following processes:
Attention:
1. What did the teacher do to attract the class's attention?
2. How did the teacher introduce the new content? Was it linked to a previously learned concept?

Retention:
1. As the new skill was modeled did the teacher point out key characteristics or steps?
2. Did the teacher think out loud, modeling the cognitive process as he or she proceeded?

Reproduction:
1. Were students given opportunities to try the new skill?
2. Did the teacher provide feedback?

Motivation:
1. How was the skill introduced? Did the teacher explain how it would be useful later on?
2. Were students provided with reinforcement as they practiced the skill?

Types of Modeling:
1. What types of modeling do you see displayed in the classroom (e.g., direct, symbolic, synthesized, abstract)? Provide specific examples.

Modeling Outcomes:
1. Describe the modeling outcomes you see (e.g., environmental enhancement effect, response facilitation effect).

Attention/Perception

Classroom Observation: Observe a classroom lesson and interview the teacher afterwards to clarify your observations. During the observation ask yourself the following questions?

1. How did the lesson begin? Were all students drawn into the lesson? Did the lesson maintain student attention?
2. How successful were these strategies?
3. What other strategies does the teacher use to gain and maintain student attention?
4. Was there a problem with student inattention? If so, describe the problem. What appears to be the reason for the problem?
5. What did the teacher do to check the students' perceptions? Did any of the students appear to be misperceiving the teachers materials?

Working Memory

Classroom Observation: Observe a lesson to determine how the teacher accommodates limitations of short-term or working memory. As you observe, ask yourself the following questions:

1. How long does the teacher talk before pausing and asking questions to connect material? How does this relate to developmental characteristics of students?
2. What visual aids (e.g., chalkboard, overhead, charts) does the teacher use to supplement the oral presentation? How effective are these?
3. How does the teacher identify important points in the presentation?

Long-Term Memory and Encoding

Classroom Observation: Observe a lesson and interview the teacher to determine how the teacher insures that information is stored in long term memory. Ask yourself the following questions as you observe:

1. Did the teacher involve the students in rehearsal? Describe specifically what the teacher did.
2. How active were the students during the lesson? What did the teacher do to promote the activity?
3. How did the teacher organize the information for the students? What did the teacher do that encouraged the students to organize their own information?
4. What kinds of questions did the teacher ask that encouraged the students to elaborate on what they already knew?

Metacognition

Student Interview: Interview four students (two high and two low achievers) to assess the development of their metacognitive abilities.

Meta-attention:

To determine how aware the students are of the role that attention plays in the learning process ask:

1. Where do you go when you study or have school work to do?
2. Does noise bother you when you're studying? What do you do if it does?
3. Do you ever drift off when your teacher is talking? What do you do when this happens?

Metacommunication:

To determine the extent to which the students are aware of communication as a two-way process ask:

1. How can you tell if you understand something that someone has said to you?
2. How can you tell if someone understands a message that you have said to someone?
3. What can you do if someone doesn't understand something you've told them?

Metamemory:

To determine how aware the students are of the process of memory and the role it plays in learning ask:

1. If you had a telephone number to remember to call five minutes later, what would you do? What if you had to remember it for tomorrow?

2. If I gave you a list of ten objects (like shoe, ball, tree, etc.) to study for a minute and then remember, how many do you think you could remember? How would you try to do this?
3. If you had a list of spelling (or foreign language vocabulary) words to remember for a quiz on Friday, what would you do? Why?

Diversity and Information Processing

Teacher Interview: Interview a teacher to determine the impact to student diversity on information processing in the classroom. The following are some suggested questions:

1. Can you describe the differences in background experiences that your students bring to school? Can you give me some specific examples? How does this influence their learning?
2. Have you ever used any of the following to accommodate students' background diversity? If so, can you give me an example?
    *   Assessed their background knowledge prior to a lesson
    *   Assessed student perceptions of new material through questioning
    *   Provide background experiences when they are lacking
    *   Use the background experiences of peers to augment the backgrounds of others

Chapter 8: Cognitive Views of Learning: Applications

Concept and Relationships Among Concepts

Classroom Observation: Observe a lesson in which a concept is being taught, or examine a textbook and identify a section where a concept is presented. Ask yourself the following questions:

1. How complete was the definition? Was a superordinate concept identified in the definition? Were characteristics clearly specified?
2. Were positive and negative examples provided? Did they contain characteristics that enabled students to differentiate between the two? Were positive examples familiar to students? Did the negative examples help differentiate the target concept from coordinate concepts?
3. Was the concept linked to other, related concepts?
4. Was the concept presented in context, or was it presented in isolation?
5. What did the teacher do to accommodate differences in the students' background knowledge?

Classroom Observation: Observe a class in which a principle, generalization, or academic rule is being taught. Ask yourself the following questions:

1. Was the relationship among the concepts in the principle, generalization, or rule clearly presented?
2. Was the principle, generalization, or rule applied in a real-world setting?
3. What did the teacher do to accommodate differences in the background knowledge of the students?

Study Skills

Student Interview: Interview several students to determine their knowledge and use of different study strategies. If possible, select two high and two low-achieving students and compare their responses. Ask the following questions:

1. When you're studying a chapter (e.g., social studies, science) for the first time what do you usually do to help you learn the material? Why?
2. Have you ever used any of the following strategies? When do you use them and why? Do they help?
    *   Underlining
    *   Note taking
    *   Summarizing
    *   Spatial representations (e.g., concept maps, diagramming, hierarchies)
3. Have you ever been taught any study strategies? Do you ever use them? When and why?

Problem Solving

Classroom Observation: Observe a lesson in which problem solving is being taught. Ask yourself the following questions:
1. How was the lesson introduced? Had students been introduced to problem solving before? Were the problems convergent or divergent?
2. What did the teacher do to assist students' learning during the following stages?
   - Understanding the problem
   - Devising a plan
   - Implementing the plan
   - Evaluating the results
3. What type of practice and feedback were provided?

Transfer

Teacher Interview: Interview a teacher to determine how the teacher teaches for transfer. The following are some suggested questions:
1. What specific things do you do to promote transfer? Can you give me some specific examples?
2. What are the biggest problems you have getting the students to transfer?

Chapter 9: Increasing Student Motivation

Theories of Motivation

Teacher Interview: Interview a teacher to gather information about their views of motivation. Based on the views, try to determine what aspects of their views are humanistic, behavioral, cognitive, or social learning in their orientation. The following are some suggested questions:

General Motivation to Learn:
1. What do you believe is most important for the motivation of the students you teach? What do you do to capitalize on these motivators?
2. How much of the responsibility for student motivation is yours? How much is theirs?

Behavioral Approaches:
1. How important do you think it is to praise students? How much praise do you use? Why?
2. Do you use any other kinds of rewards to motivate your students to study? Can you give me some specific examples?

Humanistic Views:
1. How important do you think it is for you to try and help students develop their self-concepts? What do you do to help students develop their self-concepts? Can you give me a specific example?
2. How important do you think it is for students to believe that teachers care about them as people? Is this part of your job? Why or why not?

Cognitive Views:
1. What do you do to capitalize on students' curiosity? Can you give me some specific examples?
2. What can teachers do to make students feel responsible for their learning? What do you do? How well does it work?

Social Learning Views:
1. What do you do to make the students feel that what their learning is important or worthwhile? Can you give me some specific examples?
2. How important do you think it is to challenge your students? Do they feel better about what they've learned when it has been challenging? Can you give a specific example to illustrate your point?

Maslow's Hierarchy of Needs

Teacher Interview: Xerox a copy of Maslow's Hierarchy of Needs, and interview a teacher. The following are some suggested questions:

1. Where on the hierarchy are most of your students? How can you tell (i.e., what specific behaviors do you observe that suggest this)?
2. How do yo adapt your teaching to accommodate the needs of your students?

Attributions

Student Interview: Interview two high and two low-achieving students to investigate their views about success and failure. Ask the following questions:

1. How well do you usually do in school? Why do you think you are doing well (or not so well)?
2. Think about the last test that you took. What kind of grade did you get? Why do you think you got that grade?
3. Do you think your grades depend most on you, such as how hard you study, or do you think they depend on something else? If something else, what?

The Model for Promoting Student Motivation

Teacher Observation: The purpose of this observation is to see if teacher expectations influence interaction patterns in the classroom. Ask the teacher to identify four high and four low achieving students. Write these students' names on two sheets of paper and observe them during an interactive instructional segment. Then, answer the following questions for each student:

Teacher Expectations:

1. Where is the student seated with respect to the teacher?
2. How often does the teacher talk to or make eye contact with the student?
3. How often is the student called on during the lesson? How much time is the student given to answer?
4. What does the teacher do when the student is unable (or unwilling) to answer?
5. What kind of praise is given for correct responses?

Classroom Climate:

Classroom Observation: Observe a classroom to determine how the following variables influence classroom climate Ask yourself the following questions:

1. Are the students orderly when they enter and leave the classroom? Are the rights of all student guaranteed by the teacher?
2. During lessons are students free to respond without fear of laughed at, ridiculed, or harassed?
3. Are students able to successfully answer most questions during learning activities? How successful are the students on their seatwork and homework?
4. Does the teacher tell the students *why* they are studying a particular topic?
5. Is the material challenging but learnable? How do you know? Cite a specific example to illustrate your point.

Instruction:

1. What did the teacher do to introduce the lesson? To what extent did it attract the students' attention?
2. How involved were the students in the lesson? What did the teacher do to promote involvement?
3. What did the teacher do to help students personally relate the information they were learning?
4. Describe the kind of feedback students are getting about their progress.

Cooperative Learning: Diversity

Teacher Interview: This exercise focuses on the extent to which cooperative learning activities help accommodate diversity. Interview the teacher to see how she organized her groups. The following are some suggested questions:

1. How did you form the teams?

2. What did you do to be sure that the groups were about equal in ability, gender and cultural background?
3. What did you do to train the students to effectively interact with each other?

Classroom Observation: Now observe the class and answer the following questions:
1. Does everyone have meaningful tasks to perform during the activity?
2. Do tasks use a variety of skills and call on a variety of knowledge?
3. Do tasks provide opportunities for all students to make contributions?
4. How does the teacher monitor the groups as they work?

Chapter 10: Managing Student Behavior

Classroom Procedures and Rules

Teacher Interview: Interview a classroom teacher to find out about the classroom procedures and rules that the teacher is using. The following are some suggested questions:
1. How did you choose the rules and procedures you're using?
2. How did you teach the rules and procedures?
3. What procedures do you feel are most important in your class (e.g., the way papers are turned in, the way students enter and leave the room)?
4. What do you do when a student doesn't follow a procedure?
5. What do you do when a student breaks a rule?

Student Interview: Interview four students. Try to select students from different segments of the class (e,g., high and low achieving, students from different ethnic or cultural backgrounds). Ask the following questions:
1. How do you feel about the rules in this class? Are they fair? What does the teacher do if you break a rule?
2. Do you think rules are important to make learning easier for you? Why do you think so?

Classroom Observation: Observe the class and answer the following questions:
1. Can all the students see the chalkboard, overhead, and other displays?
2. Can all students hear the teacher and each other? If not, what is distracting the students?
3. What does the teacher do if the students are inattentive or if they break a rule?
4. How effective is the lesson in maintain student attention? Cite specific evidence to support your assessment.

Communication with Parents

Teacher Interview: Interview a teacher to find out how the teacher and the school communicate with parents or guardians. The following are some suggested questions:
1. What does the school do to communicate with parents (e.g., back-to-school night, open house, school newsletters, packets of papers sent home)? How well do they work?
2. What do you personally do to communicate with parents? How well does it work?

Advice for New Teachers

Teacher Interview: Since classroom management is one of the most severe problems new teachers face, what advice would you give them? Be as specific as possible.

Chapter 11: Planning for Instruction

Teacher Planning

Teacher Interview: Interview an experienced teacher to find out how he or she plans. The following are some suggested questions:
1. When you're planning, how do you begin? What do you do second? Third? How does this vary with different topics?
2. Do you use state or district curriculum guides? Do they help you in your planning?
3. Do you use the teacher's edition of your text? If so, how?

4. Do you do any cooperative planning with other teachers? Why or why not?
5. When you plan, what and how much do you write down?
6. Describe your long-term plans. How are they different from daily plans?
7. Do you take affective factors, such as student motivation, into account when you plan?

Teacher Observation: Ask a teacher if you can look at some of his or her plans and then observe a lesson. As you study the plans and observe the lesson, ask yourself the following questions:
1. How detailed are the plans? What does the teacher write down?
2. How closely does the teacher follow the plan? If he or she deviates from it, why do they do so?

Individualization

Teacher Interview: Interview a teacher to determine how individual differences are accommodated in the planning process. The following are some suggested questions:
1. How do you take individual differences into account in your planning?
2. Do you use computers or other forms of technology in your classroom? If so, how do you use them?

Chapter 12: Effective Teaching

Time

Teacher Interview: Interview a teacher to determine how he or she thinks about time. The following are some suggested questions:
1. How do you decide how much time to devote to a particular topic?
2. What do you do about the "dead time" periods in your classes?
3. What do you do when you see that students aren't paying attention?
4. How can you tell if students are "getting it" when you teach?

Teacher Observation: Now, observe the teacher. Ask yourself the following questions as you observe:
1. How much time does the teacher allocate to the topic?
2. How much of the allocated time is actually devoted to instruction?
3. How did the teacher begin the lesson? Did he or she purposely do something to attract the students' attention? If so, what? How well did it work?
4. Did the teacher review during the lesson? If so, when?
5. What does the teacher do when a student "drifts off"?

Student Observation: Observe four students during the course of a lesson. (Ask the teacher to select two that are high achieving and two that are low achieving.) Seat yourself so that you can observe their faces during the lesson. Focus on each student at fifteen-second intervals and decide whether the student was attending to the lesson. A "Y" indicates yes, an "N" indicates no, and a question mark indicates that you cannot tell. At the end of the twenty-minute observation period, compute averages for each student and the group as a whole. (Engagement Rate = # of times engaged/Total # of observations.)

	Student A	Student B	Student C	Student D
Minute 1				
Minute 2				
Minute 3				
. . .				
Minute 20				

Ask yourself the following questions:
1. Did the engagement rates vary during the course of the presentation? If so, why?
2. What did the teacher do differently when the students were paying attention compared to when they were inattentive?
3. How did the attentiveness of the high and low achievers compare?

Questioning

Teacher Observation: Observe a second lesson, and devote your observation specifically to the teacher's questioning patterns. Make out a seating chart for the students. Sit in the room so you can easily see who is being called on. Every time the teacher asks a question, put a check mark by the student being called on. If the student is called on because of attempting to volunteer (such as raising a hand), put an X by the student's name. Observe the lesson and tally the teacher's questions. Then ask yourself the following questions:

1. Does the teacher call on students by name, or are students called on only when they volunteer?
2. Are all the students in the class called on?
3. Are students allowed to call out answers?
4. What does the teacher do when students are unable or unwilling to answer?
5. When the teacher asks a question, how long does he or she wait for the student to answer?
6. Does the teacher direct a similar number of questions to boys and girls? To cultural minorities and non-minorities?

Student-Student Interaction

Classroom Observation: Observe a lesson for evidence of student-student interaction. As you observe, ask yourself the following questions:

1. Does any student-student interaction—related to the learning activity—take place? If so, how does the teacher promote it?
2. Does the teacher involve the class in discussions? What does the teacher do to keep the students focused on the topic? Do the students have adequate background to conduct a meaningful discussion?

Chapter 13: Classroom Assessment

Assessment Patterns

Teacher Interview: Interview a teacher about his or her attitudes toward testing and assessment patterns. The following are some suggested questions:

1. How important do you feel testing is in the assessment of your students? Can you explain?
2. Do you usually make out your own tests, or do you use tests that come with your textbook?
3. What kinds of performance assessments do you use? Can you give me some specific examples of some that you use in your class?

Test Construction

Observation: Obtain a teacher-made test, examine its contents, and ask yourself the following questions:

1. What format was used (e.g., multiple-choice)? Most of the questions were written at what level (e.g., knowledge, comprehension)?
2. To what extent were the items consistent with the guidelines provided in your text?

Teacher Interview: Interview the teacher to gather information about the way he or she prepared the test you examined. The following are some suggested questions:

1. What were your goals in constructing the test? How were the items designed to measure different types of knowledge?
2. What did you do to be sure that the content you wanted covered was covered?
3. Did you use any kind of chart or matrix in designing the test?
4. Did you utilize a computer in any way as you designed your test?
5. How will you grade the test? Will any part of it be machine scored?

Test Administration

Teacher Interview: Interview a teacher who has recently administered a test to gather some information about the ways students are prepared for tests. The following are some suggested questions:

1. Do you do anything to help your students deal with test anxiety? If so, what?
2. Do you, or have you, taught your students specific test-taking skills? Can you describe specifically how you did this?
3. Did you have your students practice on some items similar to those that will be on the test?
4. How carefully do you supervise the students while they are taking tests?
5. Is cheating ever a problem? If so, what do you do about it?
6. When you hand tests back to the students, do you go over them? Why or why not?

Grading

Teacher Interview: Interview a teacher and get a copy of the course expectations (if available) and a copy of a sample report card. The following are some suggested questions:

1. How do tests and quizzes contribute to the final grade in your class?
2. How do you use homework and seatwork in your grading system?
3. Do you use a point or a percentage system for your grading? Why?
4. Do you use computers to help you in your grading? If so, how?

Standardized Tests

Observation: If you can, get a copy of a standardized test used in the school you're visiting. (Assure school personnel that test security will be maintained.) Also ask to see the administration manual that accompanies it. Examine the test and manual and determine the following:

1. What kind of test is it (e.g., achievement, diagnostic)?
2. What kinds of items are used and how do these relate to the test's objectives?
3. How were the validity and reliability determined?
4. What guidelines are provided for test administration? How detailed are these? Why?
5. How are test results reported?
6. How are test results used?

Diversity and Assessment

Teacher Interview: Interview a teacher to determine how student diversity influences the assessment process. The following are some suggested questions:

1. How does the diversity of student backgrounds in your class affect the assessment process?
2. Do you make any special provisions in preparing students for tests? If so, what are they?
3. Is language ever a problem for students as they take tests? If so, what do you do to accommodate the problem?